simply™

fortune telling

with

playing cards

simply™

fortune telling
with
playing cards

JONATHAN DEE

A Sterling / Zambezi Book
Sterling Publishing Co., Inc.
New York

Library of Congress Cataloging-in-Publication Data Available

2   4   6   8   10   9   7   5   3   1

Published in 2007 by Sterling Publishing Co., Inc.
387 Park Avenue South, New York, NY 10016
Copyright © 2006 by Jonathan Dee
Published and distributed in the United Kingdom solely by
Zambezi Publishing, Ltd.
P.O. Box 221, Plymouth, Devon PL2 2EQ
www.zampub.com
Distributed in Canada by Sterling Publishing
c/o Canadian Manda Group, 165 Dufferin Street
Toronto, Ontario, Canada M6K 3H6
Distributed in Australia by Capricorn Link (Australia) PTY. Ltd.
P.O. Box 704, Windsor, NSW 2756, Australia

Printed in China
All Rights Reserved

For information about custom editions, special sales, premium and
corporate purchases, please contact Sterling Special Sales
Department at 800-805-5489 or specialsales@sterlingpub.com.

Zambezi ISBN-13: 978-1-903065-51-8
ISBN-10: 1-903065-51-8
Sterling ISBN-13: 978-1-4027-2698-9
ISBN-10: 1-4027-2698-8

contents

introduction

No one really knows where playing cards originated, but they seem to have arrived in Europe during the fourteenth century. It is likely that Crusaders returning from their Middle Eastern adventures brought these and other intriguing cards and games back with them. The link between playing cards and the minor arcana of the tarot is obvious: Both decks contain four suits, and the nature of the suits in playing card decks is similar to that of the suits in tarot decks.

The four suits in playing cards and some tarot decks are as follows:

PLAYING CARDS	TAROT
Hearts	Cups, Chalices
Clubs	Wands, Rods, Staves, Sticks
Diamonds	Coins, Pentacles (from the pentagram design on the coins)
Spades	Swords (the Spanish for sword is *espada*)

Three of CUPS   Five of WANDS

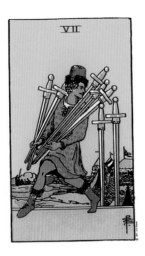

Seven of SWORDS

We now know that the roots of the minor arcana are much older than those of the major arcana, so in its way, a deck of playing cards has a provenance older than that of the modern-day tarot deck. If you want to know more about the history of the tarot, read my book *Tarot Mysteries*, and if you want to know more about the history of playing cards, read my book *Fortune-Telling with Playing Cards*.

People in Spain and Italy still play games with minor arcana cards, and they sometimes call such decks *taroc, tarocco, tarots*, or other variations on the name "tarot." It is also possible to find cards that seem to straddle the two systems. I have come across decks that carry images of acorns, cups, swords, trees, hearts, wands, spades, and other similar images, mixed with the more familiar playing-card or tarot-card symbols.

For many years, there has been a popular belief that the Joker is a leftover part of the major arcana of the tarot, and the similarity between the Fool and the Joker makes this an obvious connection. Apparently this is not the case, though, because the Joker is a recent addition that appears to have originated in America. That said, my guess is that the image of the Joker was taken from that of the Fool; if not, the similarity is an amazing coincidence.

There is a certain romance attached to playing cards. Think, for instance, of nineteenth-century riverboat gamblers who worked the steamboats on the Mississippi River, of the bewigged English noblemen who spent their evenings (and their inheritances) gambling with cards, or of the films that portrayed tough card-playing cowboys in saloons. The Internet has brought about a surge in interest in poker, and in the United Kingdom, the United States, and elsewhere, serious poker games are now televised, so a new generation of gamblers are now staring at images of playing cards and weighing up their chances.

On a more mundane note, a card game was the setting for the invention of the humble sandwich. The Earl of Sandwich was busy playing cards when dinner was announced. He was at a critical point in his game and didn't want to leave the gaming table, but he was quite hungry. When he heard that there was steak for dinner that evening, he asked a servant to put his serving of steak between two slices of bread so he could eat his meal without leaving his game.

Nowadays, there are many collectable decks of cards, such as the "Iraq war deck," emblazoned with the faces of Saddam Hussein and his cohorts. On the other hand, playing cards are also so mundane that most people have a couple of decks lying around somewhere in their houses, even if they are not particularly into card games.

Whether you have just a few or several decks of playing cards in your house, and whether your family members are avid card players or not, do remember to keep your fortune-telling cards separate from those that you and your family use for card games.

Six of PENTACLES

1

A NEW DECK

If you want to use playing cards for fortune-telling, you definite-ly need to buy a new deck, or perhaps a couple of new decks. Always purchase a new deck of cards rather than using the dog-eared cards that have been lying around your home for the past two decades. Fortunately this shouldn't be a problem, as playing cards are extremely easy to find in many different kinds of shops and stores, and they are very inexpensive.

When you have some time to yourself, unwrap your cards and take them out of the box. Hold them in your hands and imagine that you are bringing white light down from heaven or into your space from the universe. Allow the light to sur-round you and your cards for about five minutes. After this, you should start to shuffle your cards, separating them and working them back together. You can put them away after a while and then dig them out and give them another little shuffle from time to time. Before using them for fortune-telling for the first time, ask for help and guidance from your god, spiritual guides, or higher consciousness so that you use the cards well.

A nice box for
your deck of cards

When you are not using the cards, keep them in their original box, within a special bag or box, and in a safe place. Keep your cards on a shelf that is above head height. Above all, do not use your cards for games or allow others to play with them. You should respect all your tools, even if the tool in question happens to be a deck of ordinary playing cards.

NUMBERS AND TIMING

If you want to see what is likely to happen during every week of the coming year, in theory you could do so, because the fifty-two cards in a deck link with the fifty-two weeks in a year. Shuffling, laying out, and reading fifty-two cards is obviously a cumbersome thing to do, but it might be worthhwhile to experiment. Lay out several cards to represent the upcoming weeks in your future, make a note of their meaning, and check back later to see whether your "predictions" worked out.

The suits can be divided into red, which represents day, and black, which represents night. You might draw a card to see whether a particular day will be happier and more successful before or after dark.

The four suits are equivalent to the four seasons:

- Clubs   Spring
- Diamonds Summer
- Hearts   Autumn
- Spades   Winter

If you want to see when a particular event will take place, for example, pose your question and draw a card from your deck. You could ask, for instance, "When will I be able to take a vacation?" The card you draw from the deck will tell you in which season you'll be able to take a break from work.

ASTROLOGY AND THE CARDS

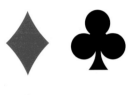

One card for
each season

Some people like to link cards to astrology, and this process can offer useful clues to the nature of certain people in a reading. It can also be used to provide more information about the nature of an event or the way it might come about. There are some quite complex connections between the cards and the decans in astrology, but the following explanation will give you some basic information:

- Hearts are associated with the water signs, Cancer, Scorpio, and Pisces.
- Clubs are associated with the fire signs, Aries, Leo, and Sagittarius.
- Diamonds are associated with the earth signs, Taurus, Virgo, and Capricorn.
- Spades are associated with the air signs, Gemini, Libra, and Aquarius.

	CLUBS (FIRE)	DIAMONDS (EARTH)	SPADES (AIR)	HEARTS (WATER)
King	Aries	Capricorn	Libra	Cancer
Queen	Leo	Taurus	Aquarius	Scorpio
Jack	Sagittarius	Virgo	Gemini	Pisces

Here are the connections between the court cards, which represent people in a reading, and the signs of the zodiac.

The astrological link can also be used as a timing device. If you want to know when something is going to happen, shuffle the cards and lay them out one by one until you draw a court card. Check the preceding table to see which

sign of the zodiac this card represents, and then use zodiac
information in the list below to check the time of year.

	SIGN	SYMBOL	DATE
♈	Aries	Ram	March 21–April 19
♉	Taurus	Bull	April 20–May 20
♊	Gemini	Twins	May 21–June 21
♋	Cancer	Crab	June 22–July 22
♌	Leo	Lion	July 23–August 22
♍	Virgo	Virgin	August 23–September 22
♎	Libra	Balance	September 23–October 23
♏	Scorpio	Scorpion	October 24–November 21
♐	Sagittarius	Archer	November 22–December 21
♑	Capricorn	Goat	December 22–January 19
♒	Aquarius	Water Bearer	January 20–February 18
♓	Pisces	Fishes	February 19–March 20

This process can be taken much further, with all fifty-two cards
being assigned to a particular decan or decanate in astrology.
If you want to know more about this technique, you can find
the information in my book *Fortune-Telling with Playng Cards*.

2

ESSENTIAL POINTS

THE COLOR OF THE READING

The most obvious and inescapable feature of any reading is the color of the cards. A predominance of red cards (Hearts and Diamonds) indicates that the reading is generally positive and that the answer to any question will be a happy one. The reverse is true if the predominant card color is black (Clubs and Spades). The result of a reading of this kind is more troublesome and worrying.

THE SUITS

A predominance of one of the four suits in the cards in a spread reveals the area of life that most concerns the questioner.

Clubs: If Clubs make up the majority of the cards in a spread, then there are new opportunities coming up, as well as encounters with new people. Friendships and the influence of people around the questioner become very important. However, there is a danger that the questioner will be too optimistic for his or her own good and take on far more than he or she can comfortably handle.

Diamonds: A majority of Diamonds in a reading indicates the importance of business matters and financial dealings. If Diamonds totally dominate the reading, then there is a danger that the questioner is too materialistic and consumed by thoughts of profit. Alternatively, this selection of cards can indicate monetary worries.

Spades: This difficult suit has a troublesome reputation, so if Spades overwhelm a spread, hard times are ahead. The suit indicates confusion and anxiety and may even warn of physical danger. Impress on your questioner that a positive mental attitude is needed to sustain him or her through these problems.

Hearts: The suit of Hearts is considered a good omen, so a lot of hearts in a spread cannot fail to be an excellent indicator of joyful times ahead. On the other hand, too many hearts may show a person who is self-indulgent, pleasure seeking, and inconsiderate toward the feelings of others.

ADJACENT CARDS

It is a general rule that more information about a card's meaning will come from the suit of the card that immediately precedes it in a spread than from the card itself. However, should any card be flanked by two cards of the same suit, then it is likely that the card's meaning will be changed in some way because it will take on some of the traits of the surrounding suit.

For instance, should a particularly troubling card, such as the Nine of Spades, meaning worries, sleepless nights, and mental anguish, be flanked by two Heart cards, the likelihood is that there is an emotional cause to the problem indicated by the Nine of Spades and that it will soon be relieved. If the dismal Nine of Spades is flanked by two Club cards, then the advice and support of friends can help, and if it is surrounded by Diamonds, then an injection of money can alleviate the problem. Conversely, should a Heart card, such as the Two, which is a card of love and attraction, be flanked by two Spades, the time lovers spend together is likely to be unpleasant and quarrelsome.

CHOOSING THE SIGNIFICATOR

Most card spreads require the selection of a card, usually a picture card, to represent the questioner. This card is referred to as the "significator." There are several ways of choosing an appropriate card for this purpose. One very popular method is to choose a card that most closely resembles the questioner in appearance, character, or coloring, or some combination of the three. For instance, the Queen of Diamonds may represent a blond, forceful woman, while the Queen of Hearts might represent a fair, sensitive, artistic woman.

Some people select a significator that symbolizes the questioner's profession or circumstances. Thus, the King of Spades might denote a professional man, while the Queen of that suit may suggest a widow or an independent woman.

Another point to bear in mind is that whichever King or Queen is chosen to be the significator, the consort of that card will represent the questioner's spouse or partner. Thus, the wife of a lawyer symbolized by the King of Spades will be depicted as the Queen of Spades, even though the woman is not a widow or independent.

Jacks usually represent youthfulness and can represent people of either gender.

REVERSED CARDS

In the descriptions that follow, I have provided a brief reversed meaning for each card. You may not want to bother with these, but if you do decide to use reversed cards, you will need to mark some of the cards so that you know which way is upright and which is reversed. Some cards, such as the Joker and the Aces, are easy to distinguish as upright or reversed.

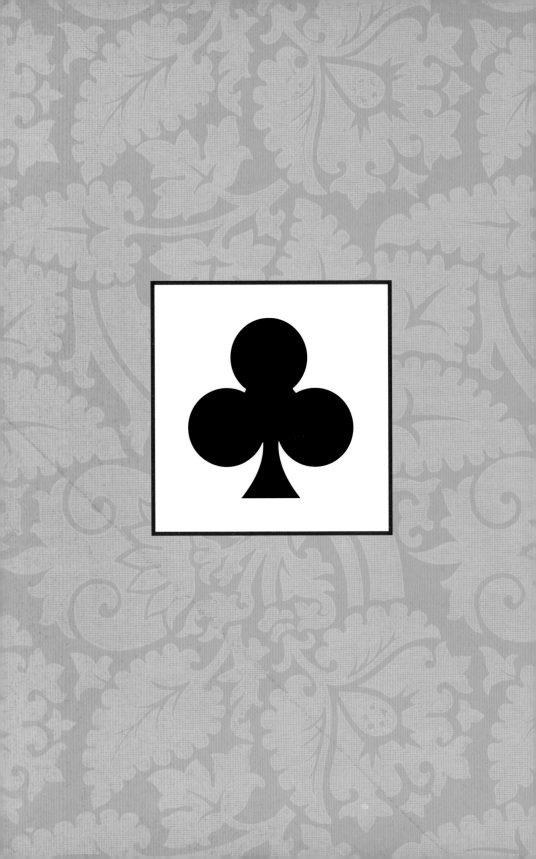

3

THE SUIT OF CLUBS

THE ACE OF CLUBS

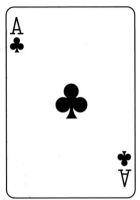

Keywords: Success, action, initiative, creativity

Quick Clues: Wealth, success, and peace of mind; also, a happy home life

The Ace of Clubs is an excellent card; it signifies a burst of energy, a new beginning, and enormous potential. This card is connected to talent and a capacity for original thought.

The Ace of Clubs can indicate a financial gain, or perhaps fame or public recognition for an achievement. This Ace brings good news, probably concerning money, but it may also signify an increase in personal status as a reward for the questioner's past efforts.

Some card readers see this Ace as symbolizing a wedding or engagement ring, and they interpret its appearance as a good omen for the questioner's love life, as well as an indicator of a lasting emotional bond.

If the Ace of Clubs is found among the first three cards in a spread, it is a sign of extraordinary talent. The questioner is likely to be in possession of unique gifts that can take him or her a long way if they are channeled in a productive fashion.

Reversed Card Meaning

The reversed card meaning is the same as the upright card meaning, but milder.

THE TWO OF CLUBS

Keywords: Potential, support, opportunity
Quick Clue: Help and support might not always take the form that the questioner desires.

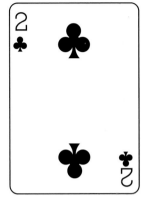

In essence, the Two of Clubs is a card of potential that suggests that opportunities and invitations are on their way. While these may seem to be unimportant initially, this will turn out to be a time of promise. The pressure is on when the Two of Clubs is present. It means that the questioner should be more self-reliant than he or she might have been in recent times. It is likely that the questioner feels that he or she has taken on too much responsibility and will count on friends and family for support through a difficult period.

It is vital that the questioner not overuse this cry for help, because this individual could wear out his or her welcome and ruin some close relationships. If these relationships start to suffer under the strain, the questioner will find that those who were previously happy to be around have become more distant. If ever there was a time for wisdom, this is it! It's time to abandon unrealistic expectations, bring things back to basics, be less heavily dependent on loved ones, and budget wisely for the future.

Reversed Card Meaning

The reversed card indicates disappointments and disagreements.

THE THREE OF CLUBS

Keywords: Feud, forgiveness

Quick Clues: Tradition says this card foretells marriage to a wealthy partner!

The Three of Clubs may be a card of potential success, but it has a definite downside. When this card is drawn, the questioner can be sure that the better he or she does, the more that success will give rise to envy, backbiting, and overt hostility, often from people who ought to know better. It may be the case that through some oversight or ill-thought-out actions, the questioner has inadvertently caused this unpleasant episode, but even so, it hardly seems just.

The next step is up to the questioner. Will he or she to take offense, react harshly, and declare the envious one an enemy for all eternity, thus creating a feud? Or will the questioner rise above the slight, prove to be a better person, and continue enjoying life and the success he or she has achieved? These are important questions for the questioner to answer.

Reversed Card Meaning

The questioner will have a partner who is able to pay his or her way but who will not be rich.

THE FOUR OF CLUBS

Keyword: Assistance
Quick Clues: Changes for the better

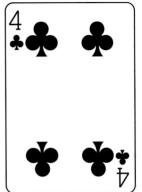

Hardened card players tended to think that a hand that contained the Four of Clubs was an ill omen. This is surprising when one considers that the card has such a good interpretation in the traditions of card reading.

When the Four of Clubs appears in a spread, the message is that help is available to the questioner, whether this assistance is actually needed or not. The implication is that the questioner's friends and colleagues respect and think well of this individual. It also means that the questioner is probably unaware of the esteem in which he or she is held. The only possible downside to the card is that the questioner may be so independent minded that he or she will refuse help when it is offered, or that this individual is somewhat emotionally repressed and finds it hard to express his or her true feelings.

Reversed Card Meaning

The reversed card indicates unreliable people around the questioner, and lies and betrayal.

THE FIVE OF CLUBS

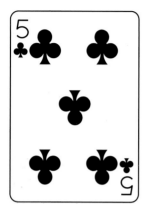

Keyword: Friction

Quick Clues: An advantageous marriage and helpful friends, but even these might fall out from time to time

Traditional interpretations of this card flatly state that the Five of Clubs means a heated argument between friends. In fact, the underlying causes of this conflict may never actually bring the questioner and his or her friends to heated words, but, nevertheless, they are troubling. The main reason for a disagreement is likely to be envy, although it is not uncommon for the people involved to flatly deny this. It is likely that one of the friends has progressed faster, earns more money, lives in a better house, drives a better car, or has something else that provokes the "green-eyed monster." The sad fact of the matter is that both parties could actually be secretly envious of each other, seeing in the other's lifestyle things that are lacking in their own.

As a card of advice, the Five of Clubs urges the questioner not to be pompous or boastful.

Reversed Card Meaning

If the questioner meets a potential lover, the encounter will result in a friendship rather than a partnership.

THE SIX OF CLUBS

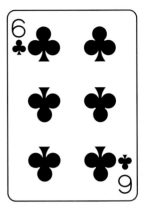

Keywords: Happy meetings

Quick Clues: Business success, especially in partnerships

The Six of Clubs is a happy card, indicating an active social life and lots of fun. More important, it also shows meetings with new people who will be a positive influence in the future. In some cases, the appearance of this card indicates a coming together of two people in a romantic sense (look to see whether the Six of Clubs is surrounded by Hearts). In another sense, the card could indicate the formation of a business partnership, or being led to the right career opportunity by a friend.

For a divorced individual, this card could point to the establishment of a new and far better relationship. For someone who is unemployed, the right job will soon turn up. If there have been family quarrels, reconciliation is now a strong possibility. In all ways, the Six of Clubs is a welcome sight in any reading, pointing to improvements in friendships, romance, and career prospects.

Reversed Card Meaning

The reversed card meaning is the same as the upright card meaning, but milder.

THE SEVEN OF CLUBS

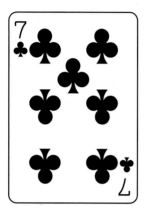

Keywords: Warning of danger ahead

Quick Clues: Happiness, joy, and prosperity, but the questioner should be careful in dealings with the opposite sex, as they will cause trouble

This has to be one of the most sexist cards in the deck! It warns that if the questioner allows a member of the opposite sex any influence in business affairs, these interests will be ruined. The only safe plan is to trust those of one's own gender—as long as there is no sexual attraction between the questioner and his or her same-gender friends!

The Seven of Clubs tells of a period of minor delays and foul-ups that cannot be avoided but have to be borne with patience and resignation. Nothing is so serious that it cannot be sorted out, unless grim cards, such as Spades, surround this card, in which case there is a definite warning of danger ahead. Even so, it might be wise for the questioner to seek some professional, even legal, advice before proceeding with his or plans.

The card might even be taken as a criticism, especially if it is one of the first three drawn. It could show that the questioner is too full of big ideas, or that this individual is great at starting projects but very poor at finishing them.

This Seven can denote a period of forced learning, in which the questioner has to take on a lot of information in a short time to protect his or her interests. It may also indicate that some people around the questioner are unworthy companions who are eroding his or her confidence.

Reversed Card Meaning

The reversed card meaning is the same as the upright card meaning, but weaker.

THE EIGHT OF CLUBS

Keywords: Peace, harmony

Quick Clues: Money comes into the questioner's life, but he or she must guard against being too open with new people who arrive on the scene.

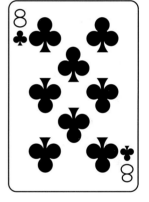

This card brings good news for those who are ground down by work and duty. The Eight of Clubs tells the questioner to take a break, that there's more to life than the rat race. It's a big world out there! This is especially true if this is one of the first three cards drawn.

The card is also an indicator of a return of peace of mind. Worry will fade. It may not disappear, but there will be a growing realization that there is more to life than the questioner's own petty concerns. If too much emphasis has been placed on material values, there will now be a change of viewpoint.

The card also suggests a journey, a voyage of discovery. The main things to be discovered, of course, are the questioner's own true self and the path to inner tranquility.

Reversed Card Meaning

The reversed card meaning indicates opposition and arguments.

THE NINE OF CLUBS

Keyword: Contentment

Quick Clues: Achievements—and if applicable, a new lover

A feeling of personal achievement and self-satisfaction is revealed by the Nine of Clubs. Whatever the questioner's goals and desires are, it is clear that he or she is a step closer to achieving them when this card appears in a reading. This is a card of progress and of making headway toward a desired goal. It may be that one more hurdle has to be dealt with before final success is achieved, yet this should not be too difficult, and the well-deserved end is in sight.

The questioner may already be aware of this, so he or she should perhaps start to look around for fresh challenges, a promotion at work, a higher level of responsibility, more status and authority, and so on.

On a social level, this card suggests enjoyment within a closely knit group of like-minded people.

Reversed Card Meaning

The reversed card meaning indicates obstacles and disagreements.

THE TEN OF CLUBS

Keywords: New beginnings

Quick Clues: Money is coming in the form of a bonus, a win, a legacy, a raise, or a business idea that takes off quickly.

The Ten of Clubs is a card of good omen regarding new beginnings. A new day has dawned, and with it comes the potential of new directions and new challenges, all of which should be embraced. Clubs are often associated with work and making an effort, so nothing will land in the questioner's lap, but all the factors are present to make a success of whatever the questioner has in mind to achieve.

This is a card of enthusiasm. It may hint of a return to the excitement and sense of adventure that is so often associated with the Ace of this suit. However, this reawakening keenness should not go to the questioner's head. If this individual concentrates solely on career and becomes a workaholic, he or she will form friendships within the working environment at the expense of family relationships and other friendships and connections.

Reversed Card Meaning

The reversed card meaning is the same as the upright card meaning, but milder and slower to materialize.

THE JACK OF CLUBS

Appearance: The Clubs Jack is usually thought of as having dark hair and eyes, though not as dark as the Jack of Spades. In personality, the Jack of Clubs is idealistic and romantic. Traditionally, this dark-haired young man is a reliable and helpful friend.

The Jack of Clubs is a faithful friend, an honest and respectable person. He may represent a young man in love. If found next to a feminine card (Hearts or Diamonds), his chances of romantic success are very good, unless that card happens to be the Jack of Hearts, in which case, a dangerous rivalry is likely. If found next to a male card (Clubs or Spades), then this Jack is a stalwart ally.

This is someone who has the questioner's best interests at heart—a thoughtful and helpful person. As usual, if this card is one of the first three cards drawn from the deck, then the Jack of Clubs either refers to the questioner or to someone who is very close to the questioner. If the questioner does not recognize the description of this character, then it is likely to represent the thoughts of a man with a dark complexion or dark hair. Since this card is quite positive, these thoughts are likely to be to the good.

Reversed Card Meaning

This young man is either unwilling or unable to help the questioner right now.

THE QUEEN OF CLUBS

Appearance: Club court cards are usually taken to represent people with dark hair and eyes. The Clubs Queen has a medium to swarthy complexion and is considered to be a lively character.

The Queen of Clubs is sociable, outgoing, and friendly. She has a lot of charm and often possesses a physical grace and elegance. However, this is only a facade, or the face she presents to the world. Mentally and emotionally, the Queen of Clubs is very shrewd indeed, and she is often a businesswoman or someone who takes to responsibility easily. This woman is adept at adjusting social situations to suit herself by her use of charm and just a little guile. This is not to say that she is coldly manipulative; she leaves that trait to the Queen of Spades. A better description of the Queen of Clubs is that she is a survivor. Tradition says that this dark-haired woman is businesslike, capable, and very attractive to the opposite sex.

She enjoys being the center of attention, but she is prone to fairly rapid mood swings that can alienate her companions. On the downside the Queen of Clubs has occasional periods of loneliness and self-pity.

This Queen has a good eye for a bargain, excellent taste, and a good eye for form and color. Consequently, her home is usually furnished to the highest and most exquisite standard.

When the Queen of Clubs is one of the first three cards dealt for a male questioner, it represents a woman who has a strong influence on his life. When it is one of the first three dealt for a female questioner, the card expresses her personality or the challenges that she is facing in her present life.

Reversed Card Meaning

This woman may be worried or may not be in a position to help the questioner. Alternatively, she may be calculating and shifty.

THE KING OF CLUBS

Appearance: In card-reading tradition, the King of Clubs has a ruddy complexion and a robust physique. He is often possessed of dark, rich brown or red hair, and brown or hazel eyes. He has an energetic and lively personality. Traditionally speaking, this is a dark-haired man. He is honest, helpful, humane, and affectionate, and he makes a faithful partner who cheers everyone up.

The King of Clubs is a helpful friend who offers support. The questioner can rely on this man. If a male questioner draws this among the first three cards, it represents him, but if the questioner is female, the card represents a male friend or relative that she respects.

If found elsewhere in a spread, it is said that if the questioner is male, then this King is likely to be a work colleague or a professional person to whom he can turn for good advice and practical help. I would suggest that this interpretation holds true for questioners of both genders these days.

As a character, the King of Clubs is quite difficult to get to know. It is likely that he has been emotionally wounded in the past and has developed some defensive barriers to prevent it from happening again. This person has wide interests and is capable of both enjoying an active social life and relishing time alone. He may be somewhat lonely and will find happiness only within a supportive relationship with someone who may not fully understand him, yet would not change him for the world.

Reversed Card Meaning

This man may be troubled, in a difficult situation, or just plain tricky and dishonest.

4

THE SUIT OF DIAMONDS

THE ACE OF DIAMONDS

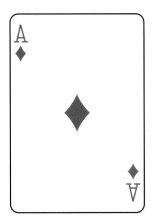

Keywords: Money, luck, communication

Quick Clues: An engagement or wedding ring; a letter bringing good news about money

The traditional meaning of this card is a message, possibly in the form of a letter, but in this age of instantaneous communication I can see no reason why the Ace of Diamonds should not represent a phone call, text message, or e-mail.

In keeping with the earthy and generally materialistic nature of the Diamonds suit, the message the Ace brings is usually connected with money. This is a positive card, so the news is likely to be good and therefore profitable. One of this Ace's subsidiary meanings is a successful and pleasing exam result.

The card is also associated with marriage, or at least the establishment of a long-term partnership. In traditional card reading, the Ace of Diamonds signifies a marriage proposal to a woman, but to a man it indicates a business proposition that has the likelihood of turning a remarkable profit.

If the Ace of Diamonds is among the first three cards in a spread, it signifies an opportunity for the questioner to use his or her abilities in a practical way that will enhance this individual's reputation and bank balance.

Reversed Card Meaning

The questioner's luck is still good, but there may be delays before things come to fruition.

THE TWO OF DIAMONDS

Keywords: Unexpected news and money
Quick Clues: A love affair that meets with opposition

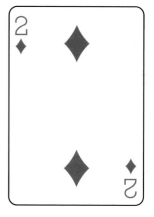

This is a card of good news, and because it is a Diamond, the glad tidings are likely to involve finances, investments, and windfalls. If an amount of money is coming the questioner's way, it isn't likely to be overly large, but it will be welcome all the same. If good news concerning money is on offer, then it is likely to come from someone close to the questioner rather than from some official source. It may be that a close friend or relative is the actual recipient of the cash, but even if this is the case, this pal won't forget the questioner, so he or she will benefit indirectly.

On the question of indirect benefits, the Two of Diamonds can be taken more symbolically, showing a karmic benefit, a reward for past efforts that the questioner has made on behalf of others.

In a question of love, this Two can show a happy, fulfilling love affair, albeit one that meets with the disapproval and suspicion of outsiders.

Reversed Card Meaning

The reversed card indicates a disappointing love affair.

THE THREE OF DIAMONDS

Keyword: Documents

Quick Clues: Legal problems, especially if the questioner is involved in a divorce; or a bad marriage or a partner who will make the questioner unhappy

There are two major themes in the Diamonds suit, and while money is the most obvious, it is closely followed by communications. The Three of Diamonds emphasizes both of these themes, so the questioner can be sure that when this card appears, important documentation will soon become an issue. The documents in question may relate to something legal or official in nature, such as a will or a contract.

A clue to the exact nature of the document may be found in the card to the immediate right of the Three of Diamonds. If no card at all appears in this position, then it is an indication of confusion, delays, and potential disputes.

Reversed Card Meaning

The reversed card indicates divorce or domestic and legal problems.

THE FOUR OF DIAMONDS

Keywords: Patient effort

Quick Clues: An inheritance or an improvement in finances

The Four of Diamonds is not an exciting card; in fact, it implies a period of slow, steady effort toward a specific goal. It is likely that this goal is financial in nature, or connected with property.

As a card of advice, the message to the questioner is to tighten his or her belt, not spend so much on luxuries and entertainment, be thrifty, work hard, and pay attention to the use of cash. This may be a bore, but the strategy will pay off in a big way. So, remember that when the Four of Diamonds appears in a reading, some sacrifices should be made, greater efforts should be made, and a shrewder outlook should be put in place. The rewards for the questioner's efforts will be very great indeed.

Reversed Card Meaning

Petty annoyances and irritations will plague the questioner.

THE FIVE OF DIAMONDS

Keywords: Business conflicts

Quick Clues: Success in business or other enterprises; if applicable, good children

The Five of Diamonds signifies matters of money and business, but the outlook is not very good. There is likely to be a difference of opinion about how exactly the questioner should move forward. The questioner and an adversary will stick to their respective points of view and behave in an extremely inflexible manner. One side of the argument is likely to be far more adventurous and impatient than the sober, cautious views of the other. A period of stalemate will be reached and it may require an intervention by an outsider to resolve the conflict.

In a more general sense, the Five of Diamonds could simply indicate a rapid series of changes that will leave the questioner wallowing for a while, until this individual gets his or her life back under control.

Reversed Card Meaning

The reversed card indicates success, but it is delayed.

THE SIX OF DIAMONDS

Keyword: Patience

Quick Clues: Problems in a marriage, especially if this is a second marriage

Although the financial picture is not likely to be a rosy one, the appearance of the Six of Diamonds suggests that there is just a glimmer of light at the end of the tunnel. This is an optimistic card, especially when related to financial or property matters. It indicates a general improvement in circumstances, and suggests that many of the questioner's anxieties will eventually fade as the world adjusts itself in his or her favor. It is at this point that the questioner's companions and family will unexpectedly offer help and advice that would have been extremely useful just a short while ago.

After this transformation has occurred, the questioner's mind is clearer and he or she can see his or her goals and how to reach them.

As a card of advice, the Six of Diamonds urges patience.

Reversed Card Meaning

The questioner shouldn't even contemplate a second marriage at this time.

THE SEVEN OF DIAMONDS

Keywords: Money warning, envy, gossip

Quick Clues: A gift or a nice surprise

This is not a good card for financial dealings. The Seven of Diamonds must be taken as a warning not to take any risks, especially with money. Therefore, speculating in the stock market, property deals, gambling, and even lending a few dollars to a friend are out. It would be wise for the questioner to put monetary plans on hold until this troublesome phase is over.

Another unfortunate aspect of the card is that it reveals that the questioner is the victim of malicious gossip that is intended to ruin his or her reputation and prospects. The usual reason for a campaign of this sort is envy, so this card can be taken as a sort of backhanded compliment, as the questioner must have done something for others to envy.

The good news is that any problems revealed by the Seven of Diamonds are likely to represent a passing phase. It will soon be over, especially if the questioner is willing to knuckle down to practicalities.

Pay attention to the cards on either side of the Seven of Diamonds, to reveal where delays and setbacks are likely to occur.

Reversed Card Meaning

The reversed card indicates waste and the loss of something valuable.

THE EIGHT OF DIAMONDS

Keywords: Material success

Quick Clues: A marriage late in life, but this is not necessarily happy or successful; plans and ideas that are worth putting into practice

The Eight of Diamonds is an excellent indicator of financial good fortune, especially if it occurs very early in a reading. Practicality is the key to success when this Eight appears. If the questioner can keep what is possible in mind, and approach all problems with a firm grip on the realities of life, then this individual will achieve all that he or she desires. This grip on reality includes health issues, for the card advises plenty of rest and recuperation after strenuous efforts.

In some cases, the Eight of Diamonds indicates an extraordinary triumph. The surrounding cards will show whether this is the case or not. If it is, then the innate practicality indicated by the card must again come into play, urging the questioner not to let success go to his or her head.

The downside to this card is that it does not bring good news concerning relationships, especially marriages or partnerships that the questioner might embark on later in life.

Reversed Card Meaning

The reversed card indicates a late marriage that is very bad indeed.

THE NINE OF DIAMONDS

Keyword: Deceit

Quick Clues: A surprise regarding money; this is good if the card is upright

On the surface, the meaning of the Nine of Diamonds is a positive one, because it clearly states that whatever they are, the questioner's wishes will come true. However, this is not as good as it seems, because this card also has connotations of danger, deceit, and unwanted complications in life. Some traditional card readers consider this card to be a warning of the appearance of a self-seeking, dishonest rogue or a traitor. The questioner needs to be on his or her guard, because all is not as it seems.

In a way, the Nine of Diamonds suggests that the questioner is indulging in self-deceit, is in denial, or is ignoring the facts, and that things (and people) are not what they seem to be. The questioner may be accepting what he or she wants to believe, rather than facing reality.

This card also hints that whatever the questioner desires should be worthwhile, honest, and beyond reproach, because if it is not, this individual will wish that he or she had never wanted it in the first place, owing to the trouble it will inevitably cause.

Reversed Card Meaning

The surprise about money mentioned in the Quick Clues section might be one the questioner doesn't want, such as an unexpected expense.

THE TEN OF DIAMONDS

Keyword: Materialism

Quick Clues: This card can bring good news about money and journeys. Tradition says that it might also denote help from a married man who lives in the countryside.

The Ten of Diamonds signifies wealth and status, but also boredom. Much has been achieved, but is this all that there is to life? That's the likely question here. The world may seem a very dull place indeed, as it is currently filled with routine and mind-numbing drudgery that is spoiling a comfortable existence.

Tens represent the end of a cycle and the beginning of a new one, so the questioner should now look for new avenues.

If this card is among the first three that are dealt, then it is likely that the questioner is feeling pretty jaded and cynical and is looking for something spiritual or meaningful to put into his or her life.

Reversed Card Meaning

There may be setbacks and delays.

THE JACK OF DIAMONDS

Appearance: The Diamonds Jack usually represents a young person of either sex, usually with rich, brown hair and dark eyes, although some say that the card symbolizes someone with red or blond hair. In older interpretations, the Jack of Diamonds represents a soldier or a man in uniform.

The Jack of Diamonds denotes a person who is confused, who may not know what to do next. This Jack gives the impression that all is well, but, in reality, he is beset by anxieties and uncertainty. Time is an important factor when this card appears. Patience and effort are required to resolve difficulties.

If the card is one of the first three drawn, then the Jack of Diamonds symbolizes the questioner or someone close to the questioner.

The appearance of the Jack of Diamonds can bring good news about money, travel in connection with business, or a promotion at work. A youngster may soon do something that will make others proud, but if the card is in an unfavorable position, then the opposite is indicated. This card can denote bad news if drawn for a woman; however, it is likely that the news will be good for a man.

Reversed Card Meaning

The Jack of Diamonds is traditionally said to be a fair-haired relative, and he may be a really difficult one, whom the questioner would be better off avoiding and keeping out of his or her home and life.

THE QUEEN OF DIAMONDS

Appearance: The Queen of Diamonds often represents a mature woman (Diamonds are often associated with age). In my experience, this Queen can suggest someone who does not look her age, who looks either older or younger than she is. Either way, she is usually fair or gray haired with a light complexion. Tradition suggests that this woman is flirtatious, sophisticated, and fond of socializing.

In traditional card reading, the Queen of Diamonds, like the King of Diamonds, has a dubious reputation. According to some, she represents a gossip who spreads rumors, and she could be a frustrated and spiteful woman. This may well have been the case in the eighteenth and nineteenth centuries, because it was very easy for a woman of ability and passion to become extremely frustrated, living in a repressive society that didn't offer her an outlet for her talents. These days, the interpretation of the Queen of Diamonds concentrates on her agile mind, her swift perceptions, and her ability to make up her mind quickly and act immediately on her decisions. Consequently, this woman can do very well in business and, in fact, any responsible position, such as raising a family. However, she is capable of becoming aggressive and is prone to creating public scenes when she is offended.

More generally, the Queen of Diamonds can be a good friend and adviser, and the reading usually indicates such a person when the card is found among the first three dealt. The Queen may represent the questioner, if she is female. More important, this card offers advice, suggesting that the questioner develop some of the more assertive traits of the Queen of Diamonds.

Reversed Card Meaning

The reversed card indicates a difficult and unpleasant woman.

THE KING OF DIAMONDS

Appearance: Traditionally, the King of Diamonds is thought of as a mature, distinguished man of military bearing. He is likely to have light or gray hair, and he often has cool blue or gray eyes. The King of Diamonds has an air of confidence and authority. Traditionally speaking, this man is obstinate or powerful, but also helpful to the questioner.

The King of Diamonds is sharp. He is extremely perceptive and shrewd, with a capacity to quickly comprehend the most complex issue. His personality is also complex, as he can be impatient and demanding. He is always on the lookout for new territories to conquer and new challenges to overcome.

This King often represents a businessman, possibly a tycoon, and he is a policy maker rather than a nuts-and-bolts details man. He has the aura of a person of authority and self-confidence, yet underneath he is not half as self-assured as he seems, and he tends to harbor self-doubt. So, he is vain and can be easily hurt if his pride is even mildly wounded.

On a more personal level, the King of Diamonds is extremely loyal to those within his circle, while he can be very dismissive of people he neither likes nor respects.

Many historical card readers disliked this card, seeing it as representing a traitor, or at least one who lacked a moral center, because he was driven by self-interest.

As a card of advice, the King of Diamonds urges care in business dealings and patience when seeking results for investments and in speculative ventures.

If the King of Diamonds is among the first three cards dealt, then it represents either the questioner or someone close to the questioner.

Reversed Card Meaning

The reversed card indicates an angry, obstinate man who may take revenge for imagined slights.

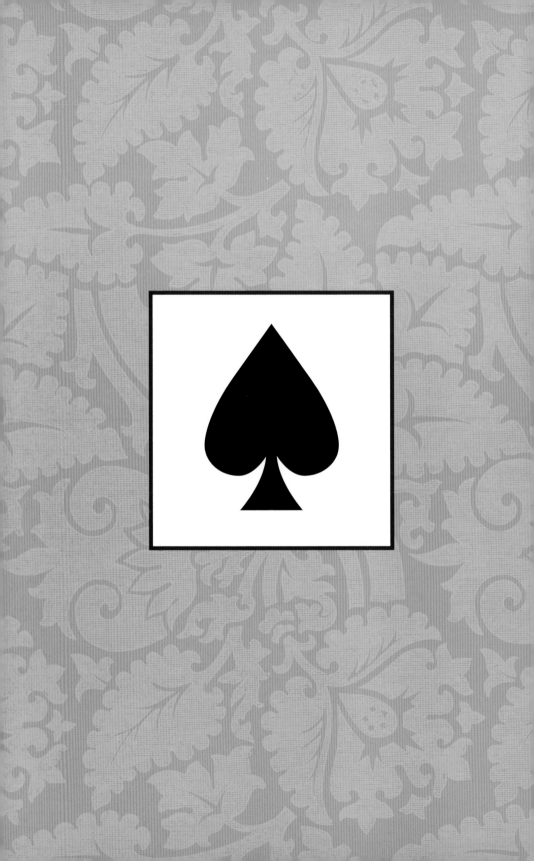

5

THE SUIT OF SPADES

THE ACE OF SPADES

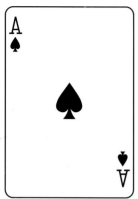

Keywords: Endings, death, challenges, ruthlessness
Quick Clues: Love affairs, passion, and obsession; friends may turn out to be deceitful

The Ace of Spades shows that this is the time to ditch the past and make a fresh start, to solve existing problems and resolve old enmities. Only when this uncomfortable process has been completed can the questioner move on to a new phase of life. Illusion is banished by the appearance of the Ace of Spades, and cozy, comforting dreams are swept away by the harsh wind of pitiless reality that will cut like a blade through the questioner's most cherished fantasies.

This Ace signifies great power. The wind of change is blowing and it cannot be resisted. It acts like a clarion call to accomplish great things. How this is to be done needs careful consideration.

This card frequently indicates the death of an idea or a way of life, so it forces the questioner to discard the outworn and useless sectors of his or her life. This can be a ruthless process, forcing an understanding and clarity on the questioner's mind. This individual may not consider these events to be welcome, but in the end, the questioner will see that the situation will work for his or her benefit.

If found among the first three cards in a reading, the Ace of Spades shows that the questioner has leadership ability and can influence others in a profound way.

Reversed Card Meaning

The reversed card indicates similar winds of change, but within the questioner's circle, not the questioner.

THE TWO OF SPADES

Keywords: Pause, tact, cautious optimism
Quick Clues: Scandal and those who gossip will make life difficult.

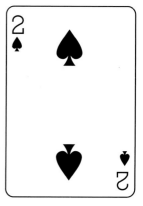

As Spades go, this is not a bad card. The Two can indicate a delicate situation, one in which the questioner feels as if he or she is treading on eggshells, trying to avoid saying the wrong thing, and paying attention to the effects of his or her words and actions on others. The problems that this card denotes are only temporary, and it may be that all the questioner needs to do is wait until the dust has settled, for a time when tempers aren't so frayed. Even so, there is room for movement. The questioner needs to be extremely diplomatic, to become a tactful go-between, smoothing out ruffled feelings so that peace gets a chance.

Although this is not a situation that the questioner would want to be in, the way in which the he or she deals with it will enhance the questioner's reputation and lead to the next cycle of his or her life. The next phase will be better and more promising.

Reversed Card Meaning

A loss or a parting in the questioner's circle is possible, due to interference by others.

THE THREE OF SPADES

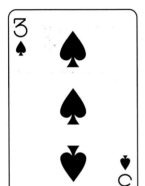

Keywords: Hasty words

Quick Clues: A wealthy partner who is fickle and unreliable

The Three of Spades depicts a frustrating situation that has gone on for a long time. Throughout this irritating period, the questioner has held his or her tongue and avoided expressing opinions, for fear of making a bad situation worse. The trouble is that this can go on for only so long; eventually the questioner's temper will reach the boiling point and words will spill out without restraint, usually in the most awkward of circumstances.

In a more general sense, the Three of Spades urges thought before action. It may indicate troubling news, or it can show that the questioner is unsure of how to react to a particular incident. Patience is the key here. When in doubt, do nothing at all! Wait and see what happens next, because the questioner can be sure that if he or she takes immediate action, the situation will become more complex and troubling.

Reversed Card Meaning

The reversed card may indicate a hasty decision, as well as a journey and a parting.

THE FOUR OF SPADES

Keywords: Peace, quiet

Quick Clues: Illness, business, and money worries will ease now.

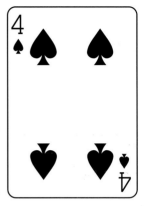

This is undoubtedly the most harmonious card in the Spades suit. This card signifies a respite from the trials and tribulations of life. It is likely that there has been a very stressful period in the questioner's life, and the appearance of the Four of Spades offers the questioner a breathing space, a chance to slow down, to reassess his or her position, and to recover depleted energies. This time is desperately necessary, if only to give the questioner's nerves a rest and to work out where he or she wants to go from here.

However, there is a hint of a warning inherent in this card's meaning. If, for whatever reason, the questioner does not intend to slow down at all, then the questioner will be forced into a period in which he or she is made to rest and to reflect on life and its direction. Thus, the Four of Spades can be indicative of stress-related ailments.

Reversed Card Meaning

Ill health, worries, and money troubles will continue for a while longer.

THE FIVE OF SPADES

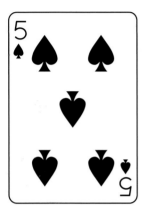

Keywords: Breaking free

Quick Clues: The questioner might have a good partner at home, but bad-tempered people outside the home environment cause problems.

The Five of Spades is a traumatic card. The events that it foretells are difficult to cope with, and they will cause doubts, self-questioning, regrets, and even some grief. It is a card that tells of separation from loved ones and from circumstances that once were comfortable but that over the course of time have become less so.

It is likely that the questioner's own decisions have caused this separation, perhaps because of feelings of being trapped, unloved, restricted in his or her actions, and generally beaten down by stress and worry. This card is sometimes associated with divorce, although a marital breakup is not the primary interpretation one should give the card in a reading.

In many ways, the card shows a flight to safety. The card to the immediate right, or at least in close proximity to the Five of Spades, should reveal whether the outcome of this flight will be good or bad.

Reversed Card Meaning

The reversed card indicates interference from outsiders and some anxiety, but also a good marriage and domestic happiness.

THE SIX OF SPADES

Keyword: Anxiety

Quick Clues: The questioner might need an increase in wages or recognition for what he or she does, but it won't be forthcoming.

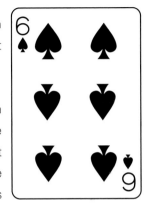

There is a proverb that says, "When poverty comes in through the door, love flies out the window," and that is the real message of this card. As usual, the Spades spell out negativity. In this case, the Six provides a warning about the questioner's domestic life, finances, and career. It looks as if disaster looms, yet this timely warning may prevent the questioner from sinking beneath the weight of his or her problems.

It is inevitable that a financial worry will have a domino effect, so something has to be done—and quickly. However, this is no cause to panic. The questioner should try to stay cool and look at the problem in a calm, logical frame of mind. If the questioner can't come up with a solution, then he or she should consult someone who can, and act on that advice.

In another sense, the Six of Spades indicates conflict and lack of cooperation.

Reversed Card Meaning

This card is much the same, whether upright or reversed. Look at surrounding cards to see whether there will be a change for the better.

THE SEVEN OF SPADES

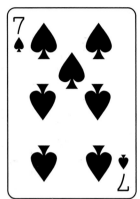

Keywords: The eye of the storm

Quick Clues: This card predicts a time of sorrow, warnings, and losses, possibly for someone the questioner knows.

An overly emotional atmosphere surrounds the questioner when the Seven of Spades is prominent in a reading. The questioner must keep cool against the odds and against all provocations. This individual may feel powerless, simply because he or she cannot get others to see his or her point of view. Actually this is a blessing in disguise, because whatever the questioner says now will be twisted and willfully misunderstood; others will make the questioner the villain, even though he or she is completely innocent of wrongdoing.

In a wider sense, the Seven of Spades warns against making far-reaching business decisions; it flatly states that the questioner doesn't know enough of what is going on and that his or her judgment is likely to be faulty. Others may be lying to the questioner about the likely success of a venture, or the questioner's own desire and imagination might make it look as though it will be more successful than it actually turns out.

That said, the card does promise great success in the future, after much persistence.

Reversed Card Meaning

The news is negative, but the effect is milder than with the upright card. There will be tears and sleepless nights.

THE EIGHT OF SPADES

Keywords: Impaired judgment
Quick Clues: Opposition from others, canceled plans, and obstacles

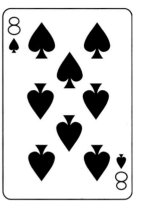

There are two sides to the Eight of Spades. On the one hand, it signifies joy, which is a rare interpretation in the Spades suit. On the other hand, as might be expected with this suit, the joy usually means that something horrible has just ended, and it really represents a sense of relief that the nastiness is over.

Another interpretation also shows that the questioner is out of trouble, but that he or she is still worrying, even though there is now nothing to worry about. The only problem remaining is a tendency to let off steam, to allow standards to slip or disappear altogether, and to totally overindulge. This may land the questioner back in troubles similar to those that he or she has recently escaped from. This kind of reaction or behavior is likely to cause misunderstandings and arguments with old friends.

Reversed Card Meaning

The reversed card indicates bad news, opposition, and troubles.

THE NINE OF SPADES

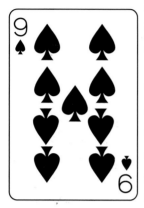

Keyword: Disappointment

Quick Clues: Domestic worries, natural disasters, destruction and war; possibly going broke

The Nine of Spades has the reputation of being one of the worst cards in the deck. Its appearance signals the end of a way of life, a collapse of previously held beliefs, and the consequent feelings of total dejection. However, this grim outlook is only part of the story, because this card, unpleasant as it is, at least provides a clean slate and an opportunity for a fresh start.

In essence, this card indicates an unwelcome forced change. The major changes that the card reveals are inevitable, and it is likely that they have been on the horizon for some time. These upheavals will make the questioner abandon selfish ways and become more thoughtful and considerate of the feelings of others.

If this card is drawn as an answer to a specific question, then that answer is a negative one. Just as the Nine of Hearts means an unequivocal "Yes," the Nine of Spades means an unequivocal "No."

Reversed Card Meaning

The reversed card meaning is still terrible, but not quite as bad as that of the upright card.

THE TEN OF SPADES

Keyword: Disillusionment

Quick Clues: Worry; feelings of being trapped or imprisoned; this card casts a cloud over any cards nearby

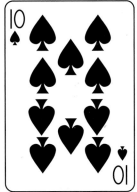

The Ten of Spades has a miserable reputation in card-reading tradition. Remember that Tens show the culmination of their respective suits, and Spades are always challenging, to say the least. The Ten of Spades represents an impassable barrier to progress. It suggests that the questioner has made great efforts but has now come to a full stop and can go no farther in this direction. This realization may come as a shock and might lead to feelings of disillusionment and pointlessness.

It is time for a change, but it is likely that the questioner will resist this necessary action because he or she has worked so hard to get to this point. Now the questioner must step back, reassess the situation, and decide which way to go from here.

Reversed Card Meaning

The reversed card meaning is the same as the meaning for the upright card, but milder.

THE JACK OF SPADES

Appearance: The Jack is often very dark, in both hair and complexion. However, many card readers have found that this Jack flies to extremes of appearance and can, therefore, be the opposite in coloring, which means very fair indeed; alternatively, this may be a person who simply has a very striking appearance and image. He is a well-meaning young man who never really gets his act together.

The Jack of Spades has a kind of roguish charm, a ready wit, and great intelligence, and is a real opportunist. He is determined and resourceful—never more so than when all seems lost. Even when things look really bad for him, the questioner can bet that he will bounce back, more cocky and audacious than ever. For the questioner to have this Jack on his or her side is a great advantage, but to have him as an enemy is very worrying indeed.

If this card is one of the first three drawn, it represents the questioner or someone very close to the questioner.

The Jack of Spades has a dubious reputation and is therefore connected to the idea of disgrace or bad behavior. It may indicate a troubled mind, betrayal in love, or a loss of liberty. This is one of the one-eyed Jacks, and one gets the impression that the Jack of Spades is a knave indeed; he often chooses to show only one side of his complex character.

Reversed Card Meaning

This Jack is a real layabout and a waste of space.

THE QUEEN OF SPADES

Appearance: This Queen is supposed to represent someone who has dark hair and eyes, but this darkness may be symbolic, reflecting an inner sorrow and a sadness that is never far from the surface. This card often represents a widow, or, in a in a wider sense, someone in a state of mourning or abandonment. Traditionally, this card symbolizes a very dark-haired or very fair-haired woman. Tradition also suggests that she is a widow or divorcée. She can be seductive and unscrupulous.

The basic interpretation of the card generally homes in on the subject of disappointment and loneliness. The card is often identified as a widow or a woman who has been left alone. However, it should not be forgotten that the Queen of Spades is capable of displaying remarkable stoicism and dignity in the face of adversity. She possesses a grim determination to survive everything that the world throws at her, and she can develop an implacable hatred for those who she thinks will stand in her way.

The Queen of Spades represents an intriguing and mysterious woman. She is reserved, cautious, and deep. She may be recovering from some emotional trauma, such as bereavement or the ending of a long-term relationship. It may be that, because of this loss, she values true friendship and will prove to be an excellent and wise adviser to those that she allows past her emotional defenses.

If the questioner is a woman and this is one of the first three cards dealt, then it is likely that it represents the questioner, and that she is in some form of mourning. If the questioner is a man, then the card, if it is one of the first three drawn, is likely to represent the questioner's mother or someone close to the questioner.

Reversed Card Meaning

The reversed card indicates a spiteful, jealous, bitter woman.

THE KING OF SPADES

Appearance: The King of Spades is usually thought of as being dark haired with dark eyes. He has a sallow complexion and an air of authority. He may be the silent type. He is certainly influential and has a strong, forceful character. Tradition says that this is either a very dark-haired or very fair-haired man who is ambitious. He is a terrific friend, but he must guard against being swindled and losing all that he has worked for.

The King of Spades is very sharp indeed. He is witty and intelligent, and he has a strong will that he is not above imposing on other people. It is fortunate that this King tends to be honest, truthful, and aboveboard in all his dealings. It may be that he represents a mature man or someone who is mature beyond his years.

The King of Spades relies on rational thinking and on logic rather than listening to the voice of intuition. He may be out of touch with his feelings, or he may find it very difficult to express them. However, the main fault of the King of Spades is his tendency to look at every situation in terms of the suit of spades

moral absolutes: black and white, right and wrong. He may have difficulty in understanding another person's point of view, and may then consider others to be stupid or obstinate simply because they cannot see things the right way—his way! This is a man of conviction who holds to high principles, even at the cost of human frailties and his own relationships.

As with other picture cards, if the King of Spades is among the first three dealt in a reading, then it is likely to represent the questioner if he is a man, or a stern man of the questioner's acquaintance, if she is a woman. It is also likely that the influence of this person has been a strong factor in the questioner's life for quite some time.

Reversed Card Meaning

The reversed card represents an ambitious, tough, selfish, and aggressive man.

6

THE SUIT OF HEARTS

THE ACE OF HEARTS

Keywords: Home, family, attraction, love, passion, creativity

Quick Clues: Joy, love, friendship, or the start of a romance

The Ace of Hearts is traditionally known as the "home card"; it is connected to those one loves. The appearance of this Ace often indicates good news, coming from or to a family member or close friend. It may signal the return of a prodigal relation, one who has been out of contact for some time. Still on the subject of family affairs, the Ace of Hearts may also show the ending of a feud or dispute and a readiness to forgive and forget.

The Ace of Hearts may show the establishment of a home with a partner, so it can indicate marriage or moving in together. In a more general sense, the Ace of Hearts shows happiness and a genial atmosphere that is shared with special people.

Of course, one aspect of the card that is impossible to ignore is its association with passion and romance. So, the card could easily indicate the beginning of a new, exciting love affair, especially if the questioner is young. On the other hand, the enthusiasm indicated by this card may be as easily directed toward an interesting new hobby or a creative enterprise of some kind.

If the Ace of Hearts is one of the first three cards drawn, it shows that the questioner is in a very emotional frame of mine, and it deals with such emotive matters as deep affections and loyalties.

Reversed Card Meaning

The reversed card can indicate friendship, rather than romance or intense passion. It might also represent the end of a love affair.

THE TWO OF HEARTS

Keywords: Happiness, contentment, simple pleasures

Quick Clues: Success, happiness, luck and prosperity; this card might predict an engagement or even a marriage

In the older traditions of card reading, the Two of Hearts can mean the beginning of love and a happy marriage, or it can indicate love letters. However, there are several other cards in the Hearts suit that mean the same thing. So, here we are looking not so much at the excitement and passion of new love as at a feeling of contentment, a quieter, less lively aspect of the emotional self. The card can mean those things, often very small things, that make one's life worth living.

This could indeed relate to peace and to those quiet moments spent with a loved one. It could just as easily refer to the pleasure a person gets when puttering around in the garden, enjoying a particularly beautiful view, listening to inspiring music, or playing with a beloved pet. These moments are often forgotten in the bustle of life, so the Two of Hearts reminds the questioner to appreciate them and gain strength from the joy of simple things.

Reversed Card Meaning

The reversed card meaning is the same as the meaning of the upright card, but delayed or surrounded by problems. Look at the surrounding cards to see what might be causing the problem.

THE THREE OF HEARTS

Keywords: Hasty promises

Quick Clues: The questioner needs to exercise caution. Rash statements will upset others.

When passions are high, words can come spilling from the lips in a gush of emotion. Whether these words are meant or not is another matter entirely. That's the message of the Three of Hearts. It may be that promises are made that, in the cold light of day, are instantly regretted. On the other hand, an argument between lovers may escalate into a full-blown quarrel, in which certain things are said that cannot easily be retracted. Thus, the Three of Hearts can indicate disappointments in love. As in the case of the Three of Spades, thoughtless words and actions can have serious and far-reaching consequences.

Reversed Card Meaning

The reversed card indicates that there may be misunderstandings and sadness, but the situation can be repaired fairly easily, perhaps after an apology.

THE FOUR OF HEARTS

Keyword: Kindness

Quick Clues: A journey or a change; if applicable, the questioner will marry later in life

The Four of Hearts is a charitable card. It signifies that the questioner will help others with no thought of reward. It shows a period when the questioner's desires take second place to the needs of others. Although this seems to imply self-sacrifice for the greater good, it won't actually be like that, because the questioner will gain personal satisfaction and a new self-knowledge from the help that he or she gives. The subsidiary meanings of the card reflect this aspect of the Four of Hearts, because it also means working in a happy and contented environment. This combines with the feeling that the questioner is doing something worthwhile, rather than simply getting on with it for the sake of a paycheck.

Reversed Card Meaning

The reversed card might relate to an irritating journey, fraught with delays and problems, or it might denote an unexpectedly awkward change in circumstances.

THE FIVE OF HEARTS

Keyword: Disappointment

Quick Clues: Money is coming to the questioner, but the questioner must take care of it because there will be jealous or unreliable people around him or her.

The Five of Hearts is the most disruptive card of this gentle suit. It has disturbing implications for relationships, and it can mean that something that was once precious is drawing to a close. It is easy to see that this could be interpreted as the end of a love affair, but it could mean that it is time to let go of a long-held ambition that once meant a lot. The good news is that the setback will be a temporary one.

As with any loss, there will be a period of mourning and self-doubt, but it won't be long before the questioner has recovered and is ready to face new challenges with renewed enthusiasm.

Reversed Card Meaning

There might be setbacks and misunderstandings, but they will be less disruptive than in the case of the upright card.

THE SIX OF HEARTS

Keyword: Panic

Quick Clues: A generous person will help the questioner and might offer a shoulder to cry on. There will be shared confidences, unexpected propositions, and good luck.

The questioner's emotions may be worn to a frazzle, and the pressure is on. Circumstances are not easy, although this is not news, as the questioner has been aware for some time that life is not as it ought to be.

Events surrounding the questioner's family and friends will make life hard for the questioner; they may be unwilling to help this individual because they are so preoccupied with their own concerns. Because they may be able to see only their own problems, they may refuse to acknowledge that the questioner has problems as well. Others could become a drain on the questioner, both financially and emotionally.

It is obvious that the questioner needs to make sensible decisions now, but taking hasty action without due caution could make things much worse. As a card of advice, the Six of Hearts urges the questioner not to panic. He or she should remain calm and think everything through slowly and carefully. Only when the questioner has subdued his or her unruly emotions can anything practical be done.

Reversed Card Meaning

The reversed card indicates that a friend needs the questioner's help.

THE SEVEN OF HEARTS

Keywords: Lovers' tiff

Quick Clues: An unfaithful or unreliable person will be around the questioner; disturbing news

A lovers' quarrel is the most commonly accepted meaning of this card. However, unless the Seven of Hearts is surrounded by particularly grim cards, this disagreement is likely to be fairly minor, and over just as quickly as it started. The deep emotions signified by the suit of Hearts hold true, and not only will love survive, but it has never really been in any danger. Following this reasoning, the card may show a temporary parting, possibly (but not necessarily) caused by a tiff. If love isn't the issue, then it is likely that someone will let the questioner down, and a friend or colleague will turn out to be unreliable.

The Seven of Hearts shows that business matters are troublesome, and it advises against getting involved in get-rich-quick schemes or trusting shady characters. If the Seven of Hearts is among the first three cards in a spread, it is likely that the questioner is too trusting and gullible. The questioner should try to act more confident and assertive than he or she feels inside.

Reversed Card Meaning

Guard against becoming involved with slippery people.

THE EIGHT OF HEARTS

Keywords: A love gift

Quick Clues: Visits and visitors, journeys for pleasure, and meals in good company

It is said that it is better to give than to receive, but in the case of the Eight of Hearts, the questioner will receive a gift that is very welcome indeed. This need not be in the form of anything material (although it often is), but rather a sort of peace offering or a gesture of affection.

This is a card of true friendship, of healing rifts, of forgiving and forgetting; it indicates the establishment of something wonderfully emotionally fulfilling. The Eight of Hearts also implies that affection is not a one-way street, that the questioner must give something in return. In most cases, this will be done gladly, and this offer of love, peace, and friendship will be wholeheartedly accepted and reciprocated.

Reversed Card Meaning

The reversed card indicates visits to irritating people, or visitors who annoy the questioner.

THE NINE OF HEARTS

Keywords: The wish card

Quick Clues: This card is said to predict health, wealth, status, and esteem. It signifies an improvement in all circumstances.

This card is traditionally considered to be a very lucky omen. The Nine of Hearts is one of the very best cards in the deck, and this is why it is called the wish card. If this card is found in a future position in a reading, the questioner can be assured that happiness is in store, that everything is going well, and that he or she is on the right path to great satisfaction in all sectors of life. The questioner can also take pride in the fact that this new joy is well deserved. There is a feeling of karmic reward here for past good deeds.

In some ancient decks, this card carried an illustration of a knight or a mounted cavalier. The movement implied in the illustration added an element of good news or a journey that brings happiness, excitement, and novelty. Perhaps this will be a great vacation. Sometimes it is a stranger who brings good news or an opportunity for travel.

If this lucky Nine is drawn as the answer to a specific question, the answer is undoubtedly in the affirmative. Just as the Nine of Spades means an unequivocal "No," the Nine of Hearts means an unequivocal "Yes."

Reversed Card Meaning

The reversed card is still good but not perhaps as spectacularly so as in the upright position.

THE TEN OF HEARTS

Keywords: Good news

The Ten of Hearts is the card of good news. This is likely to be something totally unexpected, but it appears that the questioner might have set events in motion in the past that have brought the current and future good things into being. The cards on either side of the Ten of Hearts will reveal the nature of the glad tidings.

The only possible downside to the card is that it is likely to be so good that the questioner is in danger of becoming complacent once the pleasant surprise has worn off. There is therefore an implied warning that, while it is true that this marvelous information sets off a new cycle, the questioner should not become too self-satisfied, nor rest on his or her laurels for too long.

Reversed Card Meaning

This is a happy and joyful card whether it appears upright or reversed.

THE JACK OF HEARTS

Appearance: Good looking, with a winning smile, the Jack of Hearts can turn heads, cause weakness in the knees, and turn the coolest brain to jelly! He is said to be fair, with sparkling blue eyes, but he could also be attractive in quite another way. This character certainly makes an impression. One can only hope that his sense of honor matches his fascinating looks. Look around at the nearby cards to judge his intentions.

In the traditional children's rhyme, "the Knave of Hearts stole the tarts; he stole them right away." In card reading too this Jack is a thief; in this case, he is a thief of hearts. He could be a fickle lover or a seducer. He is undoubtedly a charmer with a knack for getting away with it, and not only being forgiven but also being loved and admired in the bargain.

This is the second of the one-eyed Jacks, so always remember that not everything is as it seems.

Although the Jack of Hearts is popularly thought of as "Cupid," and thus a card that relates specifically to love and romance, the card can also indicate a break from the normal routine, a time to put the cares of the world aside and have some fun. In this sense, it could be taken as an indication of good times to come, or as an instruction not to work so hard. This Jack says, "Leave worry for another day; enjoy yourself," and who are we to disagree?

If this is one of the first three cards drawn in a reading, it represents the questioner or someone lighthearted around the questioner.

Reversed Card Meaning

The reversed card indicates that this man may be unreliable.

THE QUEEN OF HEARTS

Appearance: The Queen of Hearts is beautiful and has an artful charm. Traditionally described as being pale and fair with stunning blue eyes, she is usually delicate and has superb presentation.

As a general rule, the Queen of Hearts takes on the role of Venus, the goddess of love, so affairs of the heart are usually the issue when this card is prominent in a reading. The questioner may need to concentrate on creative matters, or on something that he or she is trying to bring into being. In addition, a certain emotional vulnerability is revealed, especially if the questioner is female. This Queen is faithful and affectionate.

The card is considered fortunate if it is one of the first three dealt, and identifies the questioner if she is female, or the love of the questioner's life if he is male. In a wider sense, the card may stand for family affection and loyalties, especially if it is among the first three cards dealt.

The Queen of Hearts loves life and she loves to be loved. This is a good thing, because everyone who encounters her will recognize that she is a loving and lovable woman. Not always the most intelligent person, this Queen works from the heart, so she is naturally emotional and extremely intuitive, understanding and sympathetic. The Queen of Hearts loves social life, she is adept at making small talk, and she enjoys fun and laughter. She hates coarseness, ugliness, and bad taste. She may be artistically gifted with excellent fashion sense and a good eye for color and form.

Reversed Card Reading

The reversed card indicates an overmaterialistic attitude and a pleasant but lazy and greedy woman.

THE KING OF HEARTS

Appearance: In common with the other Hearts picture cards, the King is said to have fair, auburn, or light brown hair and blue, gray, or hazel eyes. In character, he is friendly, open, and warm.

This man is kind, loving, and affectionate, and he will give good advice. Traditional card readers consider the King of Hearts to be an older man, because of the maturity of his outlook and the humor with which he treats problems. However, physical age is not the issue with this card, because the King of Hearts expresses a wealth of experience, and sometimes this has been gained at a relatively young age. That said, this King is often taken to represent the questioner if he is a man, if it is found among the first three cards in a spread. Alternatively, it might represent the questioner's father or grandfather. However, the precise nature of the family relationship isn't really relevant, because it is the wisdom of the person represented by the King of Hearts that counts.

As a personality, the King of Hearts symbolizes someone with a strong character, who is fair-minded, genial, open to new ideas, and reliable. He is very emotional, and he may be conscious of this as a fault, so he may try to conceal his soft heart beneath a gruff, forbidding exterior. This concealment can never last, however, because the King of Hearts is by nature someone who laughs a lot, who can't take anything too seriously for too long.

He is likely to enjoy the good life, congenial company, funny stories, and the foibles of people. He likes humanity as a concept and is usually fun to be around—except, of course, at those moments when his tender heart is stirred by the woes of the world, but even then, it's only a phase, and soon he will laugh once more.

Reversed Card Meaning

The reversed card represents poor judgment on the questioner's part or on the part of the person represented by this card. He may look terrific, but he may also be very unreliable and a philanderer as well.

7

THE JOKER

THE JOKER

It is commonly believed that the Joker is the last vestige of the major arcana of the tarot to be found in a modern playing card deck. Many people hold the view that this mysterious card is the direct descendant of the unnumbered Fool, which both begins and ends the sequence of the twenty-two trump cards dating back to at least the fifteenth century. Alas, this is not so.

The Joker was actually invented as an addition to a standard deck of playing cards, in the United States in 1857. Its original use was as the highest trump card in the game of euchre. The card wasn't even known as the Joker at the time of its conception. Its first title was, inexplicably enough, "the Best Bower." Nevertheless, card makers soon gave this new addition the familiar motley—the cap, bells, and slapstick of the medieval jester—and in doing so may have been consciously emulating cards from an earlier era, copying the tarot Fool.

The use of the Joker in divination is optional. There are no hard-and-fast rules, no grand traditions to back it up. However, many card readers have found the Joker useful as a wild card, a chaotic influence that does not fit within the definitions of the four standard suits. In fact, many suggested interpretations of the card tend to derive from the meaning of the Fool of the tarot pack.

Most decks of cards come complete with two Jokers, although only one is necessary if you choose to use it for fortune-telling purposes.

The basic interpretation of the Joker card is one of independence, eccentricity, and a need for personal freedom. When the Joker appears in a reading, it flatly states that it is folly to believe that the questioner is in control of his or her own life or can truly predict the outcome of his or her actions. It also implies moving into unexplored territory without fearing the consequences.

In essence, this card is completely devoid of materialism. It may show that the practical virtues of modern life are no longer sufficient to fill the void in the questioner's soul. Sometimes, the card indicates that a person is about to embark on a spiritual quest, either inwardly by questioning all previously held assumptions or outwardly into the wide world, taking a journey of discovery that will lead into the unknown. In the past, and in some religions even now, the idea might be one of taking time out to make a pilgrimage to a special place.

If the Joker is found early in a reading or in a position that represents the questioner, it is likely that this individual is already a spiritually evolved person but is somewhat at odds with his or her surroundings. This individual is never petty, small-minded, or prone to greed or jealousy. The questioner is free to follow his or her heart.

Reversed Card Meaning

In a more negative sense, the Joker's lack of materialistic values may warn the questioner to be less of a fool and to take more notice of his or her own interests. As the Joker is one card that has a definite upright and reversed position, this interpretation can be used for a reversed Joker reading.

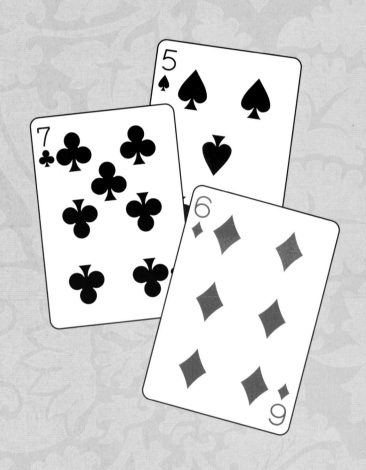

8

CARD COMBINATIONS

Playing cards can be read singly or in combination with other cards, and there are two approaches to this practice. The simplest and most effective way is to look at groups of cards that fall close to each other and see whether they link together to tell some kind of story; nevertheless, traditional card readers do take the trouble to learn the many combinations that exist. Here are some to use as a reference when you do your card readings. Any combination of cards found in a spread takes on extra significance, and it often provides an extra level of meaning to the reading.

ACES

Four Cards

A completely new and much better way of life is in store. The career is especially well starred. This combination is a very good indicator of success in all areas of life.

Three Cards

This combination represents success and help for the questioner, as well as good news and good luck. Enthusiasm and energy, new opportunities, and growing self-confidence are indicated.

Two Cards

Partnership—possibly a marriage—is indicated by this combination. The questioner may hear unusual news.

TWOS

Four Cards

This combination suggests oversensitivity, a hint of guilt, and a need to be discreet.

Three Cards

Expect happy times spent in company with loved ones, filled with great conversation, sharing thoughts, and sharing ideas.

Two Cards

Talk things over with others; don't act entirely alone.

THREES

Four Cards

The questioner would not be wise to listen to gossip, or to believe everything that he or she hears.

Three Cards

A great deal of new information will come the questioner's way. This could be an indication of education in the widest sense, academic study, or a more personal revelation.

Two Cards

Creative ventures are well starred.

FOURS

Four Cards

Plan carefully and work out the next move. This combination may signal a departure from anything that has been previously attempted.

Three Cards

This combination suggests overcoming an obstacle to progress. It can denote a chance to recuperate before new challenges are undertaken.

Two Cards

The questioner can ask for, and receive, good, practical advice.

FIVES

Four Cards

This combination is an indicator of many choices. Difficult decisions have to be made.

Three Cards

The questioner needs to escape from difficult circumstances. This may show a rising sense of panic that could lead to unwise actions. A cool head would be a great advantage at this time.

Two Cards

Life is not easy now, but a problem shared is a problem halved.

SIXES

Four Cards

This combination suggests a restful period, which is a pleasant respite, even though it does not advance the questioner's more practical interests.

Three Cards

Friends and colleagues will provide the questioner with a new opportunity.

Two Cards

There is plenty of work to do, but it will go well and the results will be good for the questioner and for his or her loved ones.

SEVENS

Four Cards

This combination denotes solitude and feelings of isolation. This introspective period will help clarify many issues for the questioner. The questioner may have enemies around, and there will be disputes, scandals, and conspiracies to contend with.

Three Cards

Some people seem to be against the questioner, but this individual must ignore other people's opinions and hold to his or her course, even though there are temporary problems. There may be illness in the family.

Two Cards

One active enemy will be around the questioner, but he or she will overcome problems, achieve success, and fulfill goals.

EIGHTS

Four Cards

This combination indicates temporary financial and business worries, but also some pleasant trips, during which the questioner spends time with friends.

Three Cards

Family problems and romantic troubles are indicated. It is best to postpone decisions until better times come along. Expect an improvement in monetary prospects, because the questioner will do something positive to ease the financial burden.

Two Cards

This combination suggests worry. A desire for love is also present, but it is accompanied by disappointment, as love will not come along yet.

NINES

Four Cards

This combination denotes good luck and unexpectedly good events. This is an excellent indicator of luck, although it would be best to be humble, as others will tend to resent the questioner's success.

Three Cards

This combination indicates success; most things will go well. Good health, happiness, and an unexpected accolade or a change of attitude for the better are expected. This may apply to those around the questioner who have been critical in the past.

Two Cards

Reasonable success is indicated. There are important documents to deal with.

TENS

Four Cards

Expect change for the better all around. This combination marks the end of an era, which is a good thing, and indicates a clean slate and the start of a new, exciting project.

Three Cards

This combination denotes money, improvement of circumstances, and finances. This may indicate a windfall for some
and the final repayment of a loan for others.

Two Cards

Money or a debt repaid is suggested by this combination.

JACKS

Four Cards

Expect disputes and quarrels amongst immature people,
and noisy parties that upset the neighbors.

Three Cards

There may be some quarreling, and the questioner may be
called on to calm down a heated situation.

Two Cards

This combination suggests argument and discussion.
Someone has bad intentions toward the questioner.

QUEENS

Four Cards

This combination suggests scandal, but also social activity. For a man, four Queens show that he may be embarrassed or compromised by his associates. For a woman, there will be backstabbing and spite among female acquaintances.

Three Cards

Backbiting and nasty remarks will upset the questioner, but things are looking up, because the questioner will soon receive invitations and will make some new female friends who will prove to be influential in the future.

Two Cards

There is some minor gossip to deal with. Also expect an interesting meeting with a female friend.

KINGS

Four Cards

Expect great success, achievement, and inheritance. For a man, high achievement, added responsibilities, and the respect and admiration of others are indicated. For a woman, this combination is not so good, indicating jealousy within a relationship and conflict between men.

Three Cards

This combination suggests success and important business meetings that will benefit the questioner. This is a good combination for both men and women. For men, it denotes true friendship and the help and support of one's peers. For women, three Kings show the possibility of romance and an enjoyable social life.

Two Cards

Some success and good business partnerships are indicated.

A quick guide to the most basic combinations

	FOUR CARDS	THREE CARDS	TWO CARDS
Aces	Great success and a completely new way of life; an especially well-starred career	Success and help to the questioner; good news and luck	Partnership, possibly a marriage; unusual news
Kings	Great success, advancement, inheritance	Success; important business meetings that will benefit the questioner	Some success; good business partnerships
Queens	Scandal, but also social activity	Backbiting and nasty remarks coming to the questioner; also, invitations	Some minor gossip; also, an interesting meeting with a female friend
Jacks	Quarrels; also, noisy parties	Some quarrelling	Argument and discussion; someone has bad intentions toward the questioner
Tens	Change for the better all around	Money; improvement of circumstances and finances	Money, a debt repaid
Nines	Good luck, unexpected good events	Success; most things will go well; good health; happiness	Reasonable success; important documents to deal with
Eights	Problems, troubles, worry; short trips to see friends	Family problems, love troubles; it is best to postpone decisions until better times come along	Worry; a desire for love, but disappointment, as love will not come along yet
Sevens	Several enemies; disputes, scandal, conspiracies	Some people seem to be against the questioner now; illness	One active enemy, but the questioner will overcome problems, reach success, and achieve goals

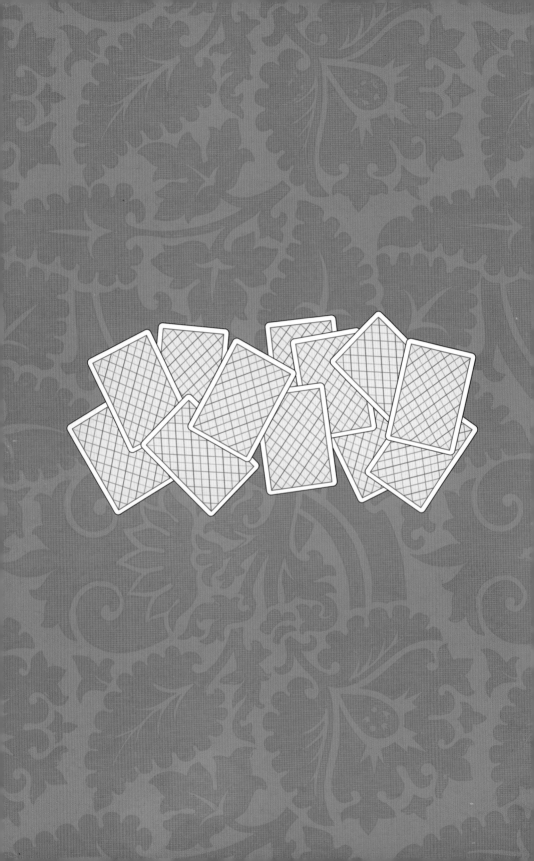

9

READING THE CARDS

°Whatever the spread you use, there are a couple of stages to go through before interpreting the individual cards. The first, and most obvious, thing to notice is the color of the reading, remembering that a preponderance of red cards denotes a positive reading, while a majority of black cards shows at least some negativity. The second stage involves keeping an eye out for meaningful combinations of cards, such as three Jacks, four Aces, three Twos, and so on. The third stage is to read the cards in sequence, using the rules of the positions in your chosen spread.

Many layouts can be used, including any that you find in a book on the tarot, or even the runes. If you wish, you can use the cards in conjunction with astrology, numerology, or the Kabala. If you use tarot cards or any other type of fortune-telling cards, you might like to try the spreads in this book with those cards too.

THE SINGLE-CARD SPREAD

The Single-Card Spread is the simplest spread of all, because it consists of one card from which the reader draws an interpretation. It still requires a calm and passive state of mind and seems to work best when a specific question is asked. I have known some card readers to use this method like a daily newspaper horoscope, to get a general indication of the day ahead.

Single-Card Spread

Example: I have just asked a friend to draw one card for me. The card that came up was the Two of Hearts. This shows that she is surrounded by love and affection, and that she might receive love letters or gifts from those who love her.

Alternatively, she might spend some time with her hobbies, with her dog, or in her garden. Vicki is happily married and her birthday is coming around, so those who love her will buy her gifts. She also says that she intends to spend more time in her garden.

THE THREE-CARD SPREAD

The Three-Card Spread is a little more detailed than the Single-Card Spread. The cards are shuffled and cut as usual, and three cards are laid in a row.

Read the cards from left to right, with A representing the past, B the present, and C the future. This spread is a good indicator of general trends, but the small number of cards in the spread means that the reading cannot be too specific.

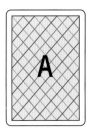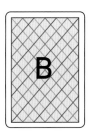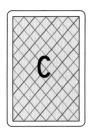

Three-Card Spread

Example: The cards drawn in order are the Ace of Clubs, Two of Diamonds, and Ten of Spades.

The Ace of Clubs indicates that the questioner has received good news in the recent past, and it also shows that he or she has enormous potential. Since it is the first card in the reading, it signifies that the questioner is a person of great talent, and this could take this individual a long way if he or she learns to channel his or her talents correctly.

The present is represented by the Two of Diamonds, which is another card of good news, indicating a windfall or some other kind of material good fortune. It may also show that there are indirect benefits to the questioner because of another person's luck. The card also reveals that fate or karma is working beneficially in the questioner's life.

The immediate future looks troublesome, owing to the presence of the Ten of Spades. This card reveals that the questioner is about to reach the end of a long-drawn-out phase. The individual may be disillusioned and somewhat bitter, because life has not provided what the questioner thinks he or she deserves. On a brighter note, the card signals that now the questioner has a blank slate and can begin something totally new.

THE MAGIC SQUARE

The Three-Card Spread can be extended into the Magic Square of nine cards. This spread can be used to add more detail to the sometimes bland responses given by the previous spread.

Magic Square Spread

Choose a court card to represent the questioner, this card is called the *significator*. Then deal three rows of three, making nine cards in all. Remove the central card and replace it with the significator. Now read each row in turn. The top row symbolizes the background to the situation, while the middle row shows the questioner's own influence upon it. The bottom row shows what the others are doing or how the situation will work out in the long run, whichever appears to be more appropriate.

THE DATE OF BIRTH SPREAD

The basic Three-Card Spread is very adaptable. In this variation, a method of card counting is used, based on the questioner's date of birth, to find three cards that will answer a specific question.

The full deck is shuffled and cut in the usual way while the questioner thinks of the issue at hand. The reader then deals the number of cards corresponding to the day of the month on which the questioner was born. For example, if the questioner was born on the tenth day of any month, the reader chooses the tenth card.

Once this is done, the reader then deals the number of cards corresponding to the questioner's month of birth; if it is April, the fourth card is chosen, if it is December, the twelfth card is chosen.

A little basic numerology comes into play now, to find the card corresponding to the questioner's birth year. Add together all the digits of the questioner's year of birth. Let's say it was 1981: $1 + 9 + 8 + 1 = 19$. Next: $1 + 9 = 10$. Continue the process: $1 + 0 = 1$. Therefore, the questioner's birth year corresponds to the very first card that is to be dealt.

So if a questioner's birth date was August 9, 1975, the first card to be chosen is the ninth dealt, as this corresponds to the day of birth. The cards are dealt again and the eighth is chosen, corresponding to August, the eighth month. Then the digits of the birth year are added: $1 + 9 + 7 + 5 = 22$; $2 + 2 = 4$. The cards are dealt again and the fourth card is chosen.

THE LONDON SPREAD

I named this configuration the "London Spread" because a friend who was living in London, England, at the time demonstrated it for me. It seems easy because there is no specific shape to the spread, but it requires more instinct and intuition than most other spreads. It is best to do this one slowly and to take plenty of time over the interpretation. Once you have learned the meanings of the cards, you might find this spread very useful, especially if you learn to switch your conscious brain off and allow yourself to go into a slightly meditative state when you interpret the cards.

Ask your questioner to shuffle the cards and then spread them out in rough lines, facedown on the table. Then ask the questioner to select fifteen cards and to place them in a random, shapeless arrangement, faceup on the table. As you read the cards, make a mental note of those that touch each other or that are close to each other. The cards that are close to each other link together in a kind of psychic connection. For instance, if a court card and a card relating to love are close to each other, the meanings of these two cards connect in the person's life.

After giving the initial reading, go through the whole process again, using twenty-one cards, and see what develops from the first reading. It is always interesting to note which cards turn up in both spreads.

London Spread

In my experience, playing cards are always read in the upright position. Some card readers use only thirty-two cards, removing the lower-numbered cards from the deck before the reading begins.

THE RECITATION SPREAD

The Recitation Spread takes time to do, but it creates a kind of meditative and slightly trancelike effect in both reader and questioner. This process may help to bring an intuitive or spiritual aspect to the reading.

After the preliminary shuffling and cutting, the reader should take the full deck and deal each card in turn while reciting the following: "Diamond, Club, Heart, Spade, Picture" (include the Joker as a picture card).

If the card dealt is the same as the word spoken, then this card is put aside to form part of the reading. For instance, when the reader says, "Diamond," and the Four of

Diamonds turns up, this card is part of the reading, but if that card were to appear when the reader says, "Spade," it would not become part of the reading.

The same rule applies for picture, or court, cards; in short, the court cards are allowed to become part of the reading only when the word "Picture" is said. In effect, this makes the court cards into a temporary fifth suit.

Go through the entire deck in this fashion, while following the formula "Diamond, Club, Heart, Spade, Picture" in strict rotation. By the time you have reached the end of the deck, you should have several cards placed in a row, ready for interpretation.

In a sample reading using this method, the following fifteen cards were chosen:

Example: Three of Diamonds, Five of Hearts, King of Spades, Four of Diamonds, Two of Spades, Five of Diamonds, Two of Clubs, Ace of Spades, Queen of Diamonds, Jack of Hearts, Ace of Clubs, Queen of Clubs, Two of Hearts, Seven of Diamonds, Six of Clubs.

The usual rules of card grouping apply: The predominant suit is Diamonds, suggesting that practical or financial issues are the central issue of the reading. The main color of the

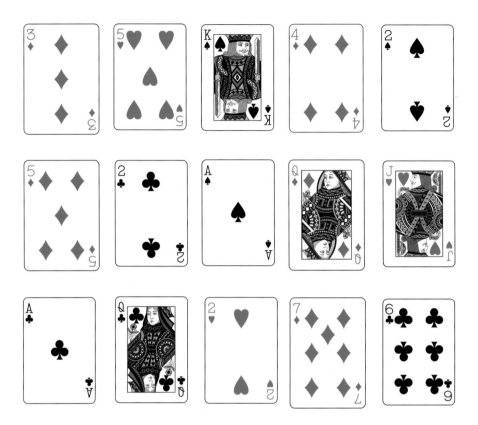

Recitation Spread

reading is red, and there are two Aces, two Queens, three Twos, and two Fives. There are eight red cards and seven black cards. After these cards are interpreted according to their grouping, the individual cards are then read in sequence.

THE HORSESHOE SPREAD

Otherwise known as the Bohemian Spread, the Horseshoe Spread is a good general pattern and also is useful for answering specific questions. The full deck is shuffled and cut as usual, then spread out on the tabletop in the shape of a fan. The questioner selects seven cards from anywhere in the fan and hands them to the reader, who places them facedown in the following pattern:

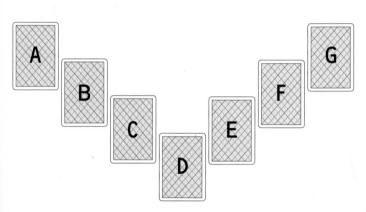

Horseshoe
Spread

Card A   Past influences that have a bearing on the present
Card B   The choices that the questioner now faces
Card C   What the questioner desires or fears
Card D   The challenges the questioner must face
Card E   Help or hindrances
Card F   Friends and foes
Card G   The outcome

THE CELESTIAL CIRCLE

The Celestial Circle is traditionally used as a birthday, or annual, reading. No specific question is required, because each card reveals the prevailing influences throughout a month (beginning at the current month, even if it is the last day of that month). The thirteenth card must be placed in the center to give a general indication of fortune throughout the year.

The reader must interpret the thirteenth card by its suit alone, so if it is a Club card, the outlook for the coming year concerns the recognition of efforts and achievements. If it is a Diamond card, the main concern is material and financial. Spades indicate a difficult time, while a Heart signifies a happy, emotionally fulfilling year ahead.

After the deck is shuffled and cut in the usual way, twelve cards are laid out like a clock face, and the reader interprets each card for a month in the coming year, moving clockwise and starting from the top.

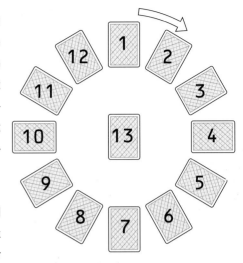

Celestial Circle

THE HOROSCOPE VARIATION SPREAD

The Horoscope Variation Spread can be adapted into a horoscope. The cards are still laid out in a circle with an "overall" card in the center, but the reader must follow the rules of astrology, with the first card on the left of the circle in the nine o'clock position. The remaining cards are laid out in a counterclockwise direction.

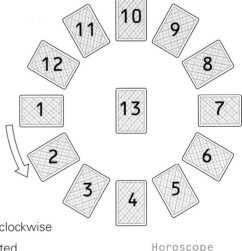

The reader starts with the card on the left and works his or her way around in a counterclockwise manner, until all the cards have been interpreted.

Horoscope
Variation Spread

Card 1   The questioner's personality and self-expression

Card 2   Values and possessions

Card 3   Siblings, early education, and local travel

Card 4   Background, family life, and home

Card 5   Romance, creativity, and children

Card 6   Work, health, and habits

Card 7   Long-term relationships and rivalries

Card 8   Sex and psychology

Card 9   Beliefs, philosophy, and distant travels

Card 10   Career, ambitions, and status

Card 11   Friends, hopes, and wishes

Card 12   Secrets and circumstances that are difficult or confining

Card 13   Overview and the influences of fate

THE MYSTIC CROSS

The Mystic Cross is a thirteen-card spread that requires a significator. Start by choosing a significator, using the questioner's gender, coloring, profession, or star sign as a guide—or just select the card that you feel best describes the questioner.

Twelve cards are dealt at random from the full deck, after the usual shuffling and cutting. Place the significator among them and repeat the process of shuffling and cutting.

The vertical row refers the questioner's present circumstances; the reader must interpret it from top to bottom. The horizontal row refers to outside influences that will affect the questioner's life. The reader should interpret this row from right to left.

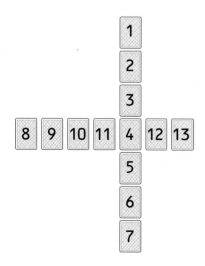

Mystic Cross

The first thing to look out for is the position of the significator. If it is found in the vertical row, it means that the questioner is in circumstances that are beyond his or her control. If the significator falls in the horizontal row, it means that the questioner is in command.

The central card at the intersection of the two rows, in position 4, is the factor around which the whole reading revolves. It is, therefore, the key to the spread and can often provide the answer that the questioner seeks. If the significator is found in this position, then anything that the questioner intends to do is the right thing.

THE TWENTY-ONE-CARD "ROMANY" READING

The Twenty-One-Card Romany reading, a traditional type of reading, is very adaptable. It is often used as a general reading at the beginning of a card-reading session, but it can also be consulted to answer a specific question.

After the deck is shuffled and cut, twenty-one cards are laid out in three rows as follows:

The top row reveals the past, most particularly the events that led up to the present circumstances. The middle row indicates the situation at present and the people who are an influence on the questioner. The bottom row denotes the future and the likely outcome.

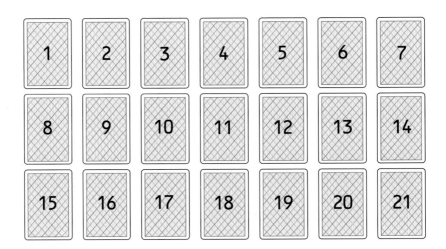

21-Card
Romany Spread

THE FAN SPREAD

Choose a significator, but just make a note of the card; leave it in the deck. Cut and shuffle the cards in the usual way, then deal thirteen cards. Check these cards to see whether the significator is present, but don't change the order of the cards. If the significator is not there, then use the Seven of the same suit that the significator came from. If neither card is present, then the reading is abandoned and the whole process begins again.

If either the significator or the Seven is present, then lay the cards out in a fan from left to right with their edges slightly overlapping. The questioner then randomly selects five additional cards from the deck, and these are laid out in a row below the fan of cards.

The cards in the fan are interpreted first. They reveal the immediate past and the current situation. There is an enhancement that you might wish to try, but if you decide that it is too involved, just read each card in turn, counting

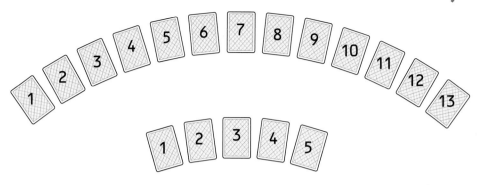

those closest to the significator (or the substituted Seven) as being the most important.

The enhancement works like this: Find the correct sequence of cards by locating the significator or its substitute and counting along toward the right until you reach the fifth card. After this card has been interpreted, count along five again to find the next card. When all the cards (with the exception of the significator or its substitute) have been read in this fashion, you can move on to the future with the five cards below the fan.

After you have read the upper, larger section of the fan, read the five "future" cards in pairs, starting at both ends of the row. Read the two ends as a pair, then the next two in from the end, and so on until you reach the last card, which you read singly. This card represents the outcome and the likely decision that will finally be reached.

COMBINED SPREADS

I have shown how a spread can be linked to astrology, because that is a very common way of reading playing cards or tarot cards. However, the cards can be laid out in a

Tree of Life design and read as per the *sephirot* of the Kabala. They can also be used with numerology, or with practically any other system you can think of.

Here is one spread I have invented specifically for this book, which goes to show just how flexible card reading can be. This reading links the cards to the seven planets that one can see with the naked eye. You can put the cards in a row, or make a design that encompasses seven cards, if you like.

The Sun—The self, children, father, fame, success

The Moon—The family, mother, home, small businesses

Mercury—Neighbors, siblings, travel, contacts, education

Venus—Young women, love, partnerships, enemies, luxury, treats

Mars—Young men, aggression, assertion, effort, energy, sex

Jupiter—Expansion, the law, higher education, spirituality

Saturn—Limitations, sickness, poverty, struggle, hard lessons

THE ELEMENTAL SPREAD

The Elemental Spread is another combined spread; this is a very easy one for those who are familiar with the elements (earth, air, water, fire, spirit). If you like, you can draw a pentagram (five-pointed star) on a large sheet of paper and lay a batch of cards on each point of the pentagram. Remember to keep your pentagram upright, with the single point at the top, for luck.

Shuffle the cards, deal three cards each into five piles, and link each pile to an element:

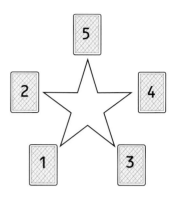

1. The bottom left point of the star is assigned to the element of earth.
2. The top left point of the star is assigned to the element of air.
3. The bottom right point of the star is assigned to the element of water.
4. The top right point of the star is assigned to the element of fire.
5. The topmost point of the star is assigned to the element of spirit.

Elemental
Spread

VARIOUS ROW SPREADS

As a break from trying out all the fancy spreads, there are many readings that one can do with a simple row of seven cards. The idea of using seven cards in this kind of spread probably stems from the belief that the number seven is lucky.

Here are a few row-based ideas that you can try for yourself. They all start with a card that represents the questioner or the questioner's situation, and many of them end with an outcome card. You can choose a significator to represent the questioner or just see which card emerges to represent the person or the situation. The first reading is rather vague, but the others are more specific.

Various Row
Spread

Spread One

1. The questioner
2. What is for the person
3. What is against the person
4. The best that can be hoped for
5. The worst that can be hoped for
6. Unexpected events
7. The outcome

Spread Two

1. The questioner or situation
2. The things that are for or against the questioner
3. How the past has influenced the person or situation
4. How the future will influence the person or situation
5. Those who will help the person
6. Those who will harm the person
7. The outcome

Spread Three

1. The questioner
2. Health
3. Wealth (or lack of it)
4. Family life
5. Love relationships
6. Career matters
7. Outcome

This spread can be adapted for each questioner and for many different scenarios. The only limit is the card reader's imagination.

Here is one that might address a situation in which the questioner is in love with someone but is not sure how the situation will work out:

Spread Four

1. The questioner (a significator would be good here)
2. The one the questioner loves
3. Any other person who might be involved
4. Influences that might have a helpful bearing on the situation
5. Influences that might have an unhelpful bearing on the situation
6. What the one whom the questioner loves really wants
7. The outcome

Here is the same spread adapted to work for a career question:

Spread Five

1. The questioner (a significator would be good here)
2. The present career situation
3. Things that are open and obvious relating to the situation
4. Things that may be going on behind closed doors, that are not obvious
5. People who might help
6. People who definitely won't help
7. The outcome

How about adapting this to a possible change of address? Well, let's try it:

Spread Six

1. The questioner
2. The bad things about his or her current home
3. What would be gained by moving
4. What would be lost by moving
5. The changes that can be expected
6. The changes that cannot be expected
7. The outcome

THE CELTIC CROSS

Any spread that a tarot reader uses can be used for playing cards. The obvious one that practically every tarot reader uses at some time or other is the Celtic Cross.

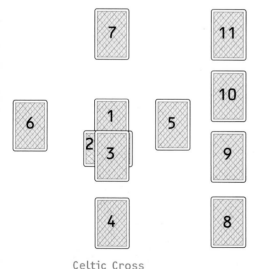

Celtic Cross

The questioner should shuffle the cards, cut them, put the deck back into one stack, and give it back to the reader. The reader then lays the cards out in the familiar Celtic Cross shape. There are some slight differences between readers as to the order that they read the cards in, so if the reader wants to change the order a little, he or she should feel free to do so.

The reader can choose a specific significator for this reading or can use a card that seems to present itself as a significator of the situation or the questioner at the time of the reading. Now you can read the Celtic Cross pattern just as you would when reading tarot cards.

1. The significator
2. The situation
3. That which is for or against the questioner
   or situation
4. The distant past
5. The recent past
6. The immediate future
7. The goal, or the best one can expect to occur
8. The questioner's influence on his or
   her environment
9. The environment's influence on the questioner
10. The questioner's hopes and fears
11. The outcome

THE PYRAMID SPREAD

In the Pyramid Spread, the cards are laid out in a pyramid shape; the pyramid can be large or small. For instance, the pyramid might have three cards at its base, two above, and a final one at the top.

When reading a pyramid spread, whether it is a small one or a large one, the reader needs to go about it in the same way. She should start by looking at the base of the pyramid and reading the cards from left to right, as this will show her the basis of the problem. As she moves up the pyramid read, she should read each row in turn from left to right to see how the situation will develop. The last card shows the eventual outcome as things stand at the moment. If the questioner is not happy with the reading, I suggest that he or

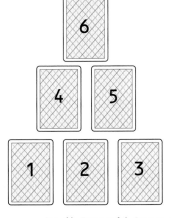

Small Pyramid Spread

she make some lifestyle changes and have another reading in a month or so.

The pyramid spread might have four, five, six, seven, or more cards at its base. It is worth experimenting with this spread to discover the size of pyramid that suits the reader best. Frankly, I find anything larger than a five-card base unwieldy.

There are differing views about how to read the pyramid spread. I like to consider the lowest row of cards as the

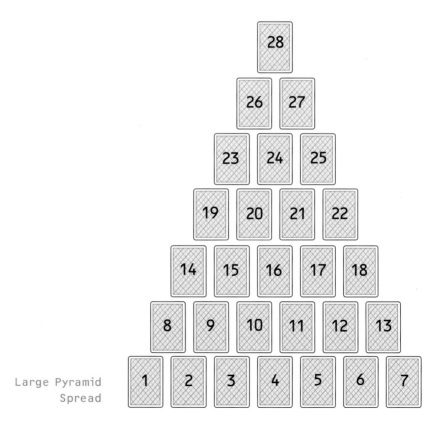

Large Pyramid
Spread

basis of the questioner's situation, so I start by reading that, then work up the pyramid to a one-card conclusion. Others prefer to take the single card at the top of the pyramid to represent the questioner's situation and then work down to a rather rounded answer. If the reader plans to read the pyramid in that way, I suggest that only a very small pyramid be used, or the reader and the questioner will become very confused.

10

SAMPLE READINGS

SAMPLE READING FOR ALICE

I have used a basic seven-card spread that is a favorite for many different kinds of card readings. Each position in the spread has its own meaning. I haven't made any attempt to read the cards in anything other than the upright position.

This reading is for a middle-aged woman named Alice. Alice's life has been difficult in recent months, as she has suffered worry, illness, and financial problems. She is also dealing with some highly unpleasant and untrustworthy people in one aspect of her life. Fortunately, Alice is happily married. She and her husband are both feeling the strain, and they need a holiday.

The Reading

A	Joker
B	Three of Diamonds
C	Ace of Clubs
D	Ace of Hearts
E	Six of Hearts
F	Two of Spades
G	Seven of Clubs

Alice's reading contains three black and three red cards, with the Joker holding the balance. Although I initially chose to read all the cards in an upright position, I couldn't help noticing that the Joker and both Aces were reversed.

Different card readers have different opinions, based on their personal experience. Some find that reversed cards tend to refer to situations that have already passed, while others see these relating to future events. I have always found that reversed cards apply to future events.

The Reading

Position A—The person
Card—The Joker

This card can symbolize a highly unconventional or eccentric person. This would not describe Alice herself, so it might suggest the behavior of those around her, and she may not be able to gauge how others will act in any given situation. The other meaning of this card is that matters are not in Alice's control, and that she needs to go with the flow. The card implies spiritual protection, so Alice can move into any new avenues that open up for her with confidence.

It is worth mentioning that when the Joker is reversed, it shows that the questioner is the type of person who does far too much for others and rarely thinks of his or her own needs. Alice says that she has done a great deal to help others in a particular situation and that she is now considering backing away and letting them get on with it.

Position B—The situation, and the things that are for or against the person
Card—Three of Diamonds
Keyword: Documents

This card relates to contracts, business, and money matters, which represent Alice's main concerns at the time of the reading. Alice agreed that this was so.

Position C—The recent past, in connection with the
content of the reading
Card—Ace of Clubs
Keywords: Success, action, initiative, creativity

Something that Alice has recently done or set in motion has been a success, and this will stand her in good stead in the future. Aces always imply new circumstances that have yet to come about, and to me, reversed cards always represent something yet to come. So, although the position relates to the past, the card is firmly set in the future!

Club cards tend to bring help from friends, and they also indicate improvements in business and financial matters. It seems that Alice is poised on the point of change in her life.

Position D—The near future, in connection with the con-
tent of the reading
Card—Ace of Hearts
Keywords: Home, family, attraction, love, passion, creativity

Alice is happily married, so home and family matters are more relevant to her than a new love affair. She says she is very happy at the news that there will be a bit more passion in her future, and she says her husband will be glad to hear that as well! The interesting thing in this reading is that both these Aces mention creativity, so that appears to be an important factor in Alice's life, and it is true that she works in a creative field.

The fact that the first three cards all indicate a fresh start suggests that whatever else comes out of this reading, the overriding factor is that Alice will soon be doing new things. An interesting circumstance is that Alice remembers a similar reading that she had many years ago, which preceded a much-needed major change for the better.

Position E—Other people's influence, whether helpful or harmful
Card—Six of Hearts
Keyword: Panic

Unusually for the suit of Hearts, this is an unpleasant card. It refers to the behavior of others as being harmful and extremely wearing on the emotions. Alice agrees that this is the crux of the matter. She says that a particular group of people with whom she has recently been dealing is totally negative, and that she has been contemplating ways of getting these people out of her orbit. The cards agree that this is a very good idea.

Bear in mind that the Joker in this reading indicated that strange (and even crazy) people are a factor in Alice's life at present.

Position F—The direction that Alice should take
Card—Two of Spades
Keywords: Pause, tact, cautious optimism

The Two of Spades in this position suggests that Alice is in a delicate situation that requires tact. Alice says that, although she would love to tell certain people what she thinks of them, and to announce to the wider world that these people are not honest or nice, the card is right. She needs to extract herself from the environment as quickly and as gracefully as she can, and then to keep her mouth firmly shut about it all.

Position G—The outcome
Card—Seven of Clubs
Keywords: Danger ahead

This card advises against taking on large projects that might be hard to finish. It also confirms that there is one person around (or perhaps more than one), who is out to erode Alice's confidence and to make her feel incompetent or stupid. The card also predicts a period of enforced learning and of taking on a lot of information in a short time in order to protect her interests.

Once again, the theme of this reading is clearly spelled out. Alice has new and important tasks ahead of her, probably with a steep learning curve involved. However, she needs to take time off for a rest before these challenges come her way. She also needs to extract herself from a particular group and to keep her opinions about them to herself. It is possible that these factors are linked, in that she needs to clear the negative group out of her life in preparation for the expansive changes that will be coming in.

Two Aces

This reading contains two Aces, which tell us that Alice will not be alone as this story unfolds. She will meet new people who will help her, and her husband will also support her initiatives.

Alice said that the reading was more in the form of advice than fortune-telling, but that there is obviously something big lurking around the corner that she cannot yet see. This is sometimes a somewhat frustrating situation, when the cards refuse to reveal certain upcoming matters. This does not mean that the reading isn't working; more likely, the cards aren't showing certain things that the questioner might be inclined to resist, or perhaps expedite, if he or she became aware of them. There are definitely times when we aren't meant to try to change the future.

SAMPLE READING FOR JACK

Jack is a man in his forties. His partner died some time ago, he is in business, and his business is not going particularly well at the moment, either. He could do with some good news.

We used a very simple spread consisting of three rows, showing three cards for Jack's past, three for his present, and three for his future.

Jack's Past

Five of Clubs
Nine of Spades
Eight of Clubs

The first card is the Five of Clubs, which carries the keyword "friction." This card denotes heated arguments, mainly due to someone else's jealousy. Jack says he has done well in the past, and this did lead to jealousy and unpleasantness from others.

The second card is the notorious Nine of Spades, which carries the keyword "disappointment." This can be a very negative card, and it definitely does portray times of great misery. This is obviously attached to the loss of his partner through cancer.

The third card is the Eight of Clubs, which carries the keywords "peace" and "harmony." This shows that, even in Jack's past, the seeds of a better future were being sown. He would come to terms with his loss, and perhaps travel for a break and in search of pastures new. He did take a good holiday and did some traveling as soon as he recovered a little from his loss.

Jack's Present

Eight of Diamonds
Six of Hearts
Ten of Hearts

The first card is the Eight of Diamonds, which carries the keyword "material success." This card suggests success and achievement, but it also warns against overdoing things and advises that Jack should rest when he can. Jack says he threw himself into work after losing his partner, and he is also rebuilding his business after several setbacks. He says he forgets to get enough rest.

The second card is the Six of Hearts, which carries the keyword "panic." This card also came up in Alice's reading. It shows that family or others might be draining Jack. He says there is a tendency for them to ask him for money whenever they are short, and while he is happy to help in times of genuine need, he is aware that some friends and relatives are taking advantage of his generosity.

The last card is the Ten of Hearts, which carries the keywords "good news." This card sets good things in motion, although it doesn't necessarily stipulate what they might be. There will be pleasant surprises and better times to come.

Jack's Future

Nine of Clubs
Queen of Hearts
Jack of Diamonds

The first card is the Nine of Clubs, which carries the keywords "a time of contentment." This shows that Jack will be happier in the future and will be able to relax with friends and loved ones. His business will prosper and he will be happy.

The second card is the Queen of Hearts. It is obvious that Jack will soon meet a new, sweet-natured partner and that he will be happy once again.

The last card is the Jack of Diamonds. It doesn't coordinate with the rest of the reading. It represents a young man who is anxious and confused. It would be worth taking this card as a significator and doing a more detailed reading over it, to see who it might be—even if Jack does not yet know him. Think about what part this character will play in Jack's future life. For instance, might this be a young person who will be attached to the new woman in Jack's life, or is this a completely new situation?

conclusion

In this book, I have kept strictly to the absolute basics of card reading, which will certainly be enough to enable you to give your friends readings and to give yourself an occasional bit of guidance. The illustrations on a deck of playing cards are far simpler than those on a tarot deck, so playing card readings appear to be much more straightforward than the tarot, but the truth is, there is far more to this subject than this book can show in a limited space.

If you decide to look further into playing card reading, you will need to investigate two completely different strands of thought. The first involves linking the cards in amazingly complex batches. Even in this very simple book, I have shown you the changes that occur when you find two, three, or four aces, or several of the same kind of court card in a single reading. The full "batching" technique is an extremely complex system that takes years to learn. In my experience, the only people who read the cards in this way are French card readers and some Gypsies.

THE CARD BATCHING METHOD

This is how the card batching system works. When a single card is paired with another, it can have a meaning completely different from the original stand-alone interpretation, and when it is paired with yet another card, the meaning changes again. Furthermore, the card can be part of a three- or four-card group that carries yet another interpretation. The following example shows you the technique. In this case, I have actually invented meanings for every batch, just to show you how the system works. We will start with the Three of Clubs, which, on its own, denotes unpleasant behavior from others, due to envy or an ongoing feud.

- The Three of Clubs with the Seven of Spades denotes painful accidents.

- The Three of Clubs with the Eight of Diamonds brings unexpected financial gain from one's career.

- The Three of Clubs with the Queen of Clubs implies that a wealthy woman is looking out for the questioner.

- The Three of Clubs with the Seven of Hearts and the Two of Spades means a journey in search of love.

- The Three of Clubs with the Five of Diamonds, the King of Hearts, and the Ten of Clubs means taking a trip up Mount Everest.

- The Three of Clubs with the Six of Spades, the Ace of Diamonds, the Jack of Hearts, and the Seven of Diamonds could mean an inheritance from an uncle who currently lives in Patagonia.

THE PICTORIAL METHOD

There are many pictorial cards with illustrations on them, such as a tree, a letter, a ship, a house, a broken heart, an arrow, and so on. These picture cards also carry illustrations of tiny playing cards at the top of each of them. These systems seem to have originated in France and then spread eastward to several eastern European countries. Some people in the United Kingdom now use cards such as these for professional readings. A particularly famous example is the Lenormand deck. Mlle. Lenormand's interpretations of the cards are completely different from standard playing card meanings.

As you can see, you can choose to use cards as an amusing pastime or for occasional guidance, or you might dive into the complexities and turn yourself into a professional reader. However you decide to read the cards, a reading always works better when combined with a healthy dose of intuition or some psychism on the part of the reader.

A final point worth mentioning is to consider the effect of your words on your questioner. Even someone who appears to be laughing at the reading, or laughing at you, can be deeply influenced and deeply upset by your words, so always think before you speak.

index

index